Dumb History

Death Trap

Dumb History

The Stupidest Mistakes Ever Made

JOEY GREEN

A PLUME BOOK

PLUME
Published by the Penguin Group
Penguin Group (USA) Inc., 375 Hudson Street, New York, New York 10014, U.S.A. • Penguin Group
(Canada), 90 Eglinton Avenue East, Suite 700, Toronto, Ontario, Canada M4P 2Y3 (a division
of Pearson Penguin Canada Inc.). Penguin Books Ltd., 80 Strand, London WC2R 0RL, England •
Penguin Ireland, 25 St. Stephen's Green, Dublin 2, Ireland (a division of Penguin Books Ltd.) •
Penguin Group (Australia), 250 Camberwell Road, Camberwell, Victoria 3124, Australia (a division
of Pearson Australia Group Pty. Ltd.) • Penguin Books India Pvt. Ltd., 11 Community Centre,
Panchsheel Park, New Delhi – 110 017, India • Penguin Group (NZ), 67 Apollo Drive, Rosedale,
Auckland 0632, New Zealand (a division of Pearson New Zealand Ltd.) • Penguin Books (South
Africa) (Pty.) Ltd., 24 Sturdee Avenue, Rosebank, Johannesburg 2196, South Africa

Penguin Books Ltd., Registered Offices: 80 Strand, London WC2R 0RL, England

First published by Plume, a member of Penguin Group (USA) Inc.

First Printing, June 2012
10 9 8 7 6 5 4 3 2 1

Illustrations from Art Explosion

 REGISTERED TRADEMARK—MARCA REGISTRADA

LIBRARY OF CONGRESS CATALOGING-IN-PUBLICATION DATA

Green, Joey.
Dumb history : the stupidest mistakes ever made / Joey Green.
p.   cm.
Includes bibliographical references.
ISBN 978-0-452-29773-9 (pbk.)
1. Errors—Humor. 2. History—Errors, inventions, etc. 3. History—Miscellanea. I. Title.
PN6231.E74G74 2012
902'.07—dc23   2011027279

Printed in the United States of America
Designed by Daniel Lagin

"Two things are infinite: the universe and human stupidity, and I'm not sure about the universe."

—ALBERT EINSTEIN

Introduction

We all make mistakes. Some of us just make much bigger mistakes than others.

Consider the story of the first emperor of China. Fearing death and determined to live forever, Qin Shihuang (259 BCE–210 BCE) sent his ministers on expeditions to find an elixir—for immortality. His court doctors and alchemists concocted a number of potions, including mercury-laden pills, which Qin Shihuang took daily, convinced they would grant him eternal life. At age forty-nine, Qin Shihuang died of mercury poisoning.

So, if you've made a really dumb mistake recently, you can take comfort knowing your faux pas probably doesn't hold a candle to some of the tremendous blunders, colossal feats of idiocy, and astounding snafus committed by others. As you'll see, some remarkably smart people have made some incredibly stupid mistakes. We all know "To err is human" and "Nobody's perfect," but now this little book of big mistakes gives you plenty of ammunition to defend yourself against those who might label you a bungler, a clod, or an incompetent goofball—as long as you don't use this book as a how-to manual.

Dumb History

Thou Shalt Proofread

In 1631, London printers Robert Barker and Martin Lucas published one thousand copies of the Bible, accidentally printing one of the Ten Commandments as "Thou shalt commit adultery."

Voting with Their Feet

During an election in 1967, the Pulvapies foot powder company ran ads in Ecuador proclaiming, "Vote for any candidate, but if you want well-being and hygiene, vote for Pulvapies." Voters in the town of Picoaza, Ecuador, with a population of four thousand, elected Pulvapies foot powder to be the new mayor.

Blundering Baghdad Betty

During the Persian Gulf War in 1991, Iraq tried to demoralize American soldiers with radio broadcasts from "Baghdad Betty," who explained: "GI, you should be home. Why? Because while you are away, movie stars are taking your women. Robert Redford is dating your girlfriend. Tom Selleck is kissing your lady. Bart Simpson is making love to your wife."

Take a Sad Song and Make It Better

On January 1, 1962, the Beatles auditioned for the Decca Record Company in London, singing fifteen songs. A few weeks later, Decca executive Dick Rowe rejected the Beatles in favor of Brian Poole and the Tremeloes because he felt "guitar groups are on the way out" and "the Beatles have no future in show business."

Child's Play

In 1974, to promote toy safety at Christmastime, the Consumer Product Safety Commission printed up eighty thousand buttons that read: "For Kids' Sakes, Think Toy Safety." The buttons—made with sharp edges, lead-based paint, and pins that came off easily and could be swallowed by a child—were immediately recalled.

Cleopatra Gets Wasted

In the 1940s, workmen cleaning a Paris museum dumped the contents of a mummy case into the sewers. The case was later identified as having contained Cleopatra's mummified remains—looted from Egypt by Napoleon.

One Way to Get a Hit

In 1920, Boston Red Sox owner Harry Frazee sold Babe Ruth to the New York Yankees for a reported $100,000 and used the money to finance the Broadway musical *No, No, Nanette*. Although *No, No, Nanette* became a hit, the Yankees won four World Series during the fifteen years Babe Ruth was in their lineup. The Red Sox did not win the World Series until 2003.

The Secret of Superiority

In 1916, Ku Klux Klan Imperial Wizard William Joseph Simmons issued an "imperial decree" declaring that the Klan's sacred book, *The Kloran*, "must not be kept or carried where any person of the 'alien' world may chance to become acquainted with its sacred contents as such." Soon afterward, Simmons decided to copyright *The Kloran* by sending two copies to the Library of Congress, where the sacred book can be read by anyone.

Mommie Dearest

According to actress Mary Astor, when Pearl Harbor was attacked on December 7, 1941, "Joan Crawford was on the set, in her chair, knitting. Someone rushed over to the set and yelled, 'The Japanese have destroyed Pearl Harbor!' Joan looked up and said, 'Oh, dear. Who was she?'"

You Ain't Nothing but a Dope Fiend

In December 1970, President Richard M. Nixon met with Elvis Presley and appointed him as an honorary federal marshal for the Drug Enforcement Administration. In 1977, Presley died of a heart attack caused by an overdose of prescription drugs, including codeine, Valium, morphine, and Demerol.

Criminal Defense

In January 1977, 25-year-old Marshall Cummings Jr., of Tulsa, Oklahoma, charged with snatching a purse at a shopping center, acted as his own defense lawyer at the trial. When cross-examining the victim, Cummings asked her, "Did you get a good look at my face when I took your purse?"

Advertising That Sucks

In the 1960s, Scandinavian vacuum manufacturer Electrolux ran advertisements in the United Kingdom, translating its slogan into English as "Nothing sucks like an Electrolux."

The Statue of Limitations

The statue of Ecuador's renowned poet José Joaquín Olmedo, in the city of Guayaquil, is actually a statue of English poet Lord Byron. The city of Guayaquil, unable to afford to commission a sculptor, purchased the statue of Byron from a London junk dealer and changed the plaque to read "José Olmedo."

The Gift That Keeps On Giving

In 1945, Soviet diplomats presented United States Ambassador W. Averell Harriman with a hand-carved wooden plaque of the Great Seal of the United States, which Harriman hung in his study. Seven years later, a Russian listening device was discovered in the plaque.

Making a Racket over
a Black Leather Jacket

In 1974, ABC network executives refused to allow the character Fonzie on the sitcom *Happy Days* to wear a black leather jacket for fear that the garment would make him look like a hoodlum. In the first few episodes of the series, Fonzie, played by Henry Winkler, wears a light gray windbreaker. Producer Garry Marshall convinced the network to let Fonzie wear a black leather jacket and boots whenever he was near his motorcycle. Marshall then instructed his staff to make sure Fonzie was with his motorcycle in every scene. Fonzie became one of the most popular characters on television, and in 1980, the Smithsonian Institution enshrined Fonzie's black leather jacket in the National Museum of American History in Washington, D.C.

The Show Must
Burn Down

On December 1, 1903, the Iroquois Theater, billed as the world's first "absolutely fireproof" theater, opened in Chicago. On December 30, a blue stage light blew out and set fire to the scenery, burning the "fireproof" theater to the ground and killing 602 people.

Snow Job

In 1970, Procter & Gamble hired model Marilyn Briggs to pose as the wholesome Ivory Snow girl, clad in a white terry cloth robe and holding a baby on the front of the Ivory Snow box. Three years later, Procter & Gamble discovered that Marilyn Briggs had become porn actress Marilyn Chambers, star of the hard-core X-rated film *Behind the Green Door.*

A Poet Should Know It

In his popular sonnet "On First Looking into Chapman's Homer," English Romantic poet John Keats incorrectly claims Spanish conquistador Hernando Cortés first looked upon the Pacific Ocean from the Isthmus of Panama. Cortés never stepped foot in Panama. Keats confused Cortés with Spanish explorer Vasco Núñez de Balboa, who spotted the Pacific from the Isthmus of Panama on September 25, 1513.

A Lake Is a Lake Is a Lake Lake

In 1859, Scottish explorer David Livingstone reached what is currently known as Lake Malawi and asked the local people what it was called. When they told him *nyasa*, he named the huge body of water Lake Nyasa. Unbeknownst to Livingstone, the word *nyasa* means "mass of waters," so the explorer actually named the body of water "Lake Lake." In 1964, the newly independent Malawi government renamed the lake Lake Malawi.

Give Us Our Daily Bread

In his 1480 fresco *Last Supper*, in the Church of Ognissanti in Florence, Italy, artist Domenico Ghirlandajo depicted bread rolls on the Passover seder table. Leavened bread is forbidden during Passover. Jesus and his disciples would have eaten matzah.

Practice What You Preach

In 1981, Tony Leone, the new Republican clerk in the Illinois House of Representatives, sent a memo to his staff members calling for accuracy in their writing. The memo contained nine grammatical, typographical, and spelling errors.

Crossing the Line

After World War I, France spent twelve years and billions of francs to build an 87-mile-long system of defensive underground fortresses along its border with Germany.

Named the Maginot Line after French war minister André Maginot, the fortresses were self-contained cities capable of housing half a million troops and linked by electric subway trains. In 1940, the Germans invaded France through its border with Belgium and captured the Maginot Line from behind.

Product Replacement

In 1982, Amblin Entertainment asked the M&M Candies division of Mars, Incorporated, in New Jersey, for permission to have Elliott, the main character in its forthcoming movie, *E.T.*, directed by Steven Spielberg, lay a trail of M&M's chocolate candies in the grass to lure an extraterrestrial. Not wanting M&M's to be associated with aliens, M&M Candies declined. Instead, Spielberg obtained permission from the Hershey Company to use Reese's Pieces, and when the movie became a runaway hit, sales of Reese's Pieces topped M&M's for the first time ever.

The Power Behind the Throne

In 1880, Emperor Menelik II of Abyssinia (now Ethiopia) ordered three electric chairs to be shipped from New York to his country, not realizing that the electric chairs required an outside electrical source. At the time, Abyssinia did not have any electrical power. Instead, Menelik used one of the electric chairs as his throne.

An Out-of-This-World Computer Crash

On December 3, 1999, a typographical error in the software code of NASA's *Mars Polar Lander* caused the spacecraft's computer to calculate that it had landed on Mars while it was still 131 feet above the planet's surface. The $165-million spacecraft shut off its engines and crashed into Mars.

The Master Race Loses Face

In 1935, German Chancellor Adolf Hitler posed for a photograph with a blond boy on his lap as the model of a pure Aryan child. The subsequent postcard sold hundreds of thousands of copies throughout Germany. The Nazis later discovered that the ideal Aryan child photographed on Hitler's lap was actually the Jewish grandson of Rabbi Wedell of Düsseldorf.

Stop and Ask for Directions

On October 25, 1964, Minnesota Viking Jim Marshall picked up a football fumbled by the San Francisco 49ers and ran sixty-six yards the wrong way into his own end zone—scoring two points for the other team.

Turning the Art World on Its Head

On October 18, 1961, New York's Museum of Modern Art opened an exhibit of the works of French impressionist Henri Matisse, accidentally displaying one of the artist's paintings, *Le Bateau* (The Boat), upside down for a total of forty-seven days. An estimated 116,000 museum visitors viewed the upside-down painting, including Matisse's son, Pierre. Wall Street stockbroker Genevieve Habert brought the mistake to the museum's attention—after visiting the exhibit for the third time.

Shaq Knows Jack

When asked by a reporter from *Sports Illustrated* if he had visited the Parthenon during his trip to Greece, basketball superstar Shaquille O'Neal replied, "I can't really remember the names of the clubs that we went to."

Toilet Troubles

In 1986, Gordon and Jasmine Geisbrecht opened the Outhouse, a restaurant in Winnipeg, Manitoba, decorated with toilet bowls around the dining room. Health inspectors shut down the restaurant for lacking sufficient bathrooms.

The Pentagon Takes a Powder

In 1989, during the U.S. invasion of Panama, Pentagon spokesmen announced that they had found fifty kilograms of cocaine in General Manuel Noriega's refrigerator. The Pentagon later admitted that the white powder was actually fifty kilograms of cornmeal intended for making tamales.

Poetic License

In his famous poem "Paul Revere's Ride," Henry Wadsworth Longfellow wrote that Revere saw one lantern light in the steeple of the Old North Church in Boston, and then rode his horse alone at midnight to Concord, Massachusetts, to warn his fellow patriots of the British invasion. In reality, Revere ordered that the lantern be lit in the steeple to signal friends in Charlestown, his "midnight ride" actually began at one a.m., and he was one of three riders on the famous journey from Boston to Concord. Along the way, the British captured Revere and forced him to walk back to Lexington without his horse.

A Matter of Interpretation

Catherine Yasinchuk spent forty-eight years in a Pennsylvania mental institution because officials did not realize that the only language she could speak was Ukrainian. In 1921, police, unable to understand Yasinchuk's hysterical babble, brought the 23-year-old to be institutionalized at Philadelphia State Hospital. When a new director was hired in 1968, the staff reviewed Yasinchuk's case and released her the following year, at the age of seventy-two.

Does Spelling Count?

In 1991, Vice President Dan Quayle and his wife sent out hundreds of Christmas cards containing a misspelled word: "May our nation continue to be the beakon of hope to the world." The following year, while helping with a spelling bee at Luis Munoz-Rivera Elementary School in Trenton, New Jersey, Vice President Quayle prodded sixth-grader William Figueroa, who had correctly spelled the word *potato* on the blackboard, to add one more letter—an *e* at the end.

Faulty Vault

On April 21, 1986, television reporter Geraldo Rivera hosted a two-hour live national broadcast from the basement of the Lexington Hotel in Chicago, where workers would open a recently discovered, sealed-off, cement-walled room, believed to be the secret vault of gangster Al Capone. The vault, blasted open after ninety minutes, contained two empty gin bottles.

Unpredictable

In 1980, televangelist Pat Robertson told his *700 Club* television show audience that the world would end in 1982. "I guarantee you by the end of 1982 there is going to be a judgment on the world," said Robertson, contradicting the Gospel of Matthew ("No one knows about that day or hour, not even the angels in heaven").

If the Shoe Fits

Whoever murdered O. J. Simpson's ex-wife Nicole Brown Simpson and her friend Ronald Goldman wore a pair of expensive Bruno Magli "Lorenzo" style shoes, leaving bloody prints near the victims at the crime scene. In a February 1996 civil lawsuit deposition, O. J. claimed, "I would have never owned those ugly-ass shoes." The next month, a photographer came forth with the negatives for a series of thirty-one photos he had taken of Simpson wearing Bruno Magli "Lorenzo" shoes at a 1993 Buffalo Bills football game.

Famous Last Words

On June 5, 1971, on *The Dick Cavett Show*, *Prevention* magazine publisher Jerome I. Rodale said, "I am so healthy that I expect to live on and on." Later in the show, while Cavett interviewed journalist Pete

Hamill, Rodale's head dropped to his chest. Cavett asked, "Are we boring you, Mr. Rodale?" Rodale had suffered a heart attack and died on the air.

Stolen Stool

On the night of November 12, 1974, Mrs. Hollis Sharpe, of Los Angeles, walked her miniature poodle and cleaned up after him with a piece of newspaper and a plastic bag. A mugger came up from behind, grabbed the bag, pushed Mrs. Sharpe to the ground, hopped in a car, and drove off.

Eat Your Ketchup

In 1981, to save money on government-subsidized school lunches, the United States Department of Agriculture announced its plan to classify ketchup as a vegetable and sunflower seeds as meat. Public ridicule prompted the Reagan administration to withdraw the plan.

Out of Hand

A nine-foot-tall statue of baseball legend Babe Ruth by artist Susan Luery, erected in front of Oriole Park at Camden Yards in Baltimore in 1995, depicts Ruth holding a right-handed baseball glove. Babe Ruth was left-handed.

A Little Rascal

On October 5, 1990, the ABC television newsmagazine *20/20* broadcast an interview with a man who claimed to be the actor who played Buckwheat in the *Our Gang* comedies. William Thomas, the actor who played Buckwheat, had died of a heart attack ten years earlier, at the age of forty-nine.

Do Your Homework

In 1971, the Texas state legislature unanimously passed a resolution commending Albert DeSalvo. State representative Tom Moore Jr. had introduced the resolution to demonstrate the carelessness with which his fellow legislators passed resolutions. He made his point: DeSalvo was the Boston Strangler.

Down the Drain with the Man with the Star

On November 20, 1980, Texaco began drilling for oil from a new rig in the middle of Lake Peigneur in Louisiana. The water immediately drained from the 1,300-acre lake, sucking eight tugboats, nine barges, five houses, a mobile home, and two oil rigs into the abandoned salt mine beneath the lake.

Smashed

On April 23, 1989, wine merchant William Sokolin, having paid $300,000 for a 1787 bottle of Château Margaux rumored to have been once owned by Thomas Jefferson, held up the bottle before three hundred wine collectors at the Four Seasons restaurant in New York City, where he hoped to sell it for $519,750. Sokolin accidentally knocked the wine bottle into a metal tray-table, smashing the bottle to pieces.

Belly Button University

At its 1990 commencement ceremony, the United States Naval Academy bestowed upon its graduates diplomas from the "Navel Academy." Navy officials failed to detect a printer's error in time to reprint the diplomas before the ceremony. The printer agreed to replace the diplomas at no cost to the government.

Special Delivery

On January 4, 1971, George Mellendorf, a soldier in Vietnam, sent a letter to President Richard M. Nixon complaining about the slow delivery of mail to the troops. Seven years later, in February 1978, the postal service delivered the letter to former president Nixon at his home in San Clemente, California.

Swedish Fish

In the early seventeenth century, King Gustavus Adolphus of Sweden ordered his navy to build the world's largest warship. On August 10, 1628, the *Vasa*, with three masts rising 165 feet and carrying five hundred sailors and soldiers, set out on her maiden voyage from Stockholm. Within ten minutes the *Vasa* keeled over, filled with water, and sank.

Not Right for the Part

In 1960, author Gore Vidal rejected Ronald Reagan for a lead role in his play *The Best Man* because he felt Reagan would not be believable as a presidential candidate.

DMV SNAFU

In 1988, Virginia's Department of Motor Vehicles issued vanity license plates to Scott and Therese Bard reading UPD WAZU. Twelve years later, the Virginia DMV deemed the license plates objectionable under its guidelines and demanded that the Bards surrender them.

Sorry, Wrong Number

In 1667, the *Wapen van Amsterdam*, a Dutch ship carrying forty crates of gold and four tons of uncut diamonds, sank. In 1983, the government of Iceland located a sunken wooden ship and spent millions of dollars to raise the *Wapen van Amsterdam*—only to bring up a German trawler that had sunk in 1903 carrying a cargo of herring.

A Red Flag

In his painting *George Washington Crossing the Delaware*, artist Emanuel Gottlieb Leutze depicts a U.S. flag that was not adopted by Congress until June 14, 1777—nearly six months after Washington crossed the Delaware River on December 25, 1776.

If He Only Had a Brain

In the 1939 movie *The Wizard of Oz*, after the Wizard bestows a diploma upon the Scarecrow, the Scarecrow points to his brain and recites: "The sum of the square roots of any two sides of an isosceles triangle is equal to the square root of the remaining side." No such theorem exists. The Scarecrow incorrectly meshes the isosceles triangle theorem with the Pythagorean theorem.

Castaway

For the 1938 film *The Adventures of Marco Polo*, movie mogul Samuel Goldwyn miscast his biggest box-office draw, actor Gary Cooper, to star as Italian adventurer Marco Polo. Throughout the film Cooper speaks with a slow Montana drawl.

That Takes Balls

While playing in the 1970 Bob Hope Desert Classic golf tournament, Vice President Spiro Agnew accidentally hit his partner, professional golfer Doug Sanders, in the back of the head with a golf ball from an errant drive. A year later, at the 1971 Bob Hope Desert Classic, Agnew accidentally sliced his first tee shot, hitting spectator G. L. Decker and Decker's wife with the same golf ball. Soon afterward, Agnew hit spectator Jacqueline Woods on the ankle with a golf ball. Remarked comedian Bob Hope at a White House dinner: "Some people think President Nixon should send Agnew to Laos with a three-wood."

Major Misnomer

On March 30, 1867, United States Secretary of State William H. Seward agreed to purchase Alaska from Russia for two cents an acre, for a total of $7.2 million. Critics, most notably *New York Tribune* editor Horace Greeley, nicknamed Alaska "Seward's Folly." Greeley wrote, "Except for the Aleutian Islands and a narrow strip of land extending along the southern coast, the country would be not worth taking as a gift." In 1896, prospectors discovered gold in the Klondike region of the Yukon Territory, creating a multimillion-dollar gold rush. In 1968, two oil companies, ARCO and Exxon, made one of the greatest oil discoveries of all time on Alaska's North Slope near Prudhoe Bay, and Alaska sold the oil and gas leases to the oil field for more than $900 million—125 times the price Seward originally paid for Alaska.

Through the Roof

Allied Roofing and Siding Company, of Grand Rapids, Michigan, cleaned snow from roofs to prevent them from collapsing from the weight of the snow. In 1979, the company's roof collapsed from the weight of snow.

All Dolled Up

In early January 2009, Ty toy company launched two new dolls, named Sweet Sasha and Marvelous Malia, as a part of their Ty Girlz collection—which included Jammin' Jenna, Happy Hillary, Bubbly Britney, and Precious Paris. Despite protests from a spokesperson for First Lady Michelle Obama, the company denied that its two new dolls were based on the Obamas' daughters. Insisting they had chosen the dolls' names because "they are beautiful names," Ty spokesperson Tania Lundeen stated, "There's nothing on the dolls that refers to the Obama girls." On February 2, Ty renamed the dolls Sweet Sydney and Marvelous Mariah.

A Major Wrinkle

In the nineteenth century, inventors created gas-heated clothes irons, but the devices, connected to gas lines, frequently leaked, exploded, and ignited fires.

Honey Don't

Utah calls itself the beehive state, despite the fact that in 2005, North Dakota led the nation in honey production with more than thirty-three million pounds, followed by California, South Dakota, and Florida. Utah tied Ohio for twenty-fifth place.

Off the Beaten Track

On April 12, 2000, the *Wall Street Journal* reported that Amtrak's online reservation system designed rather creative itineraries. "Instead of traveling from Houston to Austin via San Antonio, a twelve-hour trip," explained the *Journal*, "Amtrak's Web site planned a four-and-a-half-day journey through Jacksonville, Florida, Washington, D.C., and Chicago."

The Successful Failure

On April 11, 1970, NASA launched the *Apollo 13* rocket successfully, but 55 hours, 54 minutes into the mission, an oxygen tank exploded, causing oxygen to leak from a second tank, knocking out the command module's supply of electricity, light, and water—200,000 miles from earth. Astronauts James A. Lovell Jr., John L. Swigert Jr., and Fred W. Haise Jr. used the lunar module as a lifeboat to return safely to earth. An investigation revealed that during a test on the launchpad, the test director, in an attempt to boil off excess oxygen from a tank that had failed to empty normally, applied 65 volts of electricity for 8 hours to thermostatic switches, unwittingly welding the switches shut.

Love Is Hate

In 1975, Yasir Arafat, leader of the Palestine Liberation Organization, said, "We do not want to destroy any people. It is precisely because we have been advocating coexistence that we have shed so much blood."

Aristotle's Blunders

Greek philosopher and scientist Aristotle (384–322 BCE) incorrectly insisted that the earth is the center of the universe and the sun rotates around the earth. These ideas were accepted as fact for nearly two thousand years. Aristotle also incorrectly claimed that a heavier body falls faster than a lighter body; a body falls at a speed in proportion to its weight (meaning a ten-pound weight falls ten times faster than a one-pound weight); the space between the moon and the earth is full of air; the human embryo is produced solely from the sperm; and sound is carried to our ears by the movement of air (sound travels in waves).

Kill the Beast! Screw the Physics!

In the 1959 novel *Lord of the Flies*, by William Golding, the boys of a private boarding school, stranded on an island, use a pair of eyeglasses belonging to a boy nicknamed Piggy to start a signal fire. However, Golding tells us that Piggy is terribly nearsighted, meaning the lenses of his eyeglasses are concave, which would scatter sunlight. Only convex lenses can sufficiently focus sunlight to a point to start a fire.

Flying Off the Handle

In 1865, Lord Kelvin, president of the Royal Society, said, "Heavier-than-air flying machines are impossible."

Don't Cry for Me Argentina

In the sixteenth century, the first Spanish settlers arrived in Argentina in search of silver and gold, naming the country after the Latin word for silver—*argentum*. The settlers failed to find any silver or gold because the misnamed country lacks an abundance of mineral riches.

Hot Dam

Begun in 1960, construction of the Aswân High Dam, on the Nile River south of Aswân, Egypt, necessitated the relocation of ninety thousand people and the enormous ancient Egyptian monument at Abu Simbel—at a combined cost of $1.5 billion and fifteen years of work. Nasser Lake, created by the dam, spreads out so far that massive amounts of water evaporate, raising the concentration of salt in the Nile. Consequently, water from the river can no longer be used to irrigate some crops, and sardines from the Mediterranean Sea no longer enter the mouth of the Nile.

Prior to the dam's construction, the annual flooding of the Nile fertilized the soil in the Nile Delta, but now the dam keeps the silt in Lake Nasser, requiring Egyptian farmers to use thousands of tons of commercial fertilizer each year to replace the alluvial soils once provided naturally by the annual flooding.

A Slight Difference

During the 1948 Israeli War of Independence against the invading armies of Egypt, Syria, Jordan, Iraq, Saudi Arabia, and Lebanon, Warren Austin, U.S. ambassador to the United Nations, asked, "Why can't these Arabs and Jews resolve their differences at the conference table like good Christians?"

Driving Themselves
Out of Business

Despite the 1974 Arab oil embargo, American automobile manufacturers, convinced that Americans would always demand full-size cars, refused to build smaller, fuel-efficient vehicles. Sales of economical Japanese compact cars skyrocketed in America during the mid-1970s, nearly bankrupting Chrysler, Ford, and General Motors.

The Ultimate Sacrifice

Convinced that the sun died every night and needed human blood to give it strength to rise the next morning, the Aztecs sacrificed fifteen thousand men a year to the sun god Huitzilopochtli. The Aztec Empire, ruling Mexico during the 1400s and early 1500s, frequently started wars with other states to capture prisoners to sacrifice.

A Day at
the Races

On June 6, 1968, at the Smoky Mountain Raceway in Maryville, Tennessee, the race car driven by Buddy Baker blew out a tire on the first turn and crashed into a concrete wall. Baker was strapped onto a rolling stretcher and put in an ambulance, but the ambulance driver neglected to latch the back door. As the ambulance pulled away, the back door opened, and the stretcher, with Baker strapped to it, rolled out onto the racetrack, where race cars headed straight toward him. Luckily, Baker was rescued and brought safely to the hospital.

The Envelope Please

Actress Jane Fonda turned down the lead roles in the movies *Bonnie and Clyde* and *Rosemary's Baby* to star in the 1968 sexual science fiction movie *Barbarella*, directed by her first husband, Roger Vadim. *Bonnie and Clyde* received ten Academy Award nominations, *Rosemary's Baby* won two Academy Awards, and *Barbarella* was a box-office dud and a critical failure.

Lord Only Knows

In the 1980s, televangelist Jim Bakker reached thirteen million viewers as host of the Christian talk show *PTL Club* with his wife, Tammy Faye. The show stressed the importance of living by Christian values. In 1987, the press revealed that Bakker had an adulterous affair in 1980 with a church secretary, Jessica Hahn, paying her $265,000 to keep quiet. In 1989, after the Federal Communications Commission investigated the PTL Network, the federal government proved that Bakker had embezzled $3.7 million of the $158 million solicited from followers of the *PTL Club* for personal use. He was convicted of fraud and conspiracy and sentenced to forty-five years in prison, a sentence later reduced to six years.

Losing Faith

In February 1988, having labeled the Jim Bakker sex scandal a cancer, rival televangelist Jimmy Swaggart was photographed visiting prostitute Debra Murphree at a Travel Inn motel in New Orleans. In the July issue of *Penthouse* magazine, Murphree revealed the pornographic acts Swaggart allegedly paid her to perform for him over a year's time. According to Murphree, Swaggart was "kind of perverted . . . I wouldn't want him around my children." In April 1988, the Assemblies of God defrocked Swaggart and he resigned from the church.

Get Out of Jail, Free

On March 20, 1982, nine inmates at the newly opened, $11.2-million, computer-controlled Baltimore County Detention Center, billed as "the most modern jail in the United States," escaped by kicking out an "unbreakable" window.

Batty Bombs

During World War II, the Pentagon developed a one-ounce incendiary bomb that could be strapped to the chest of a bat and then dropped over Japanese cities, where the bat would land in a home or building and chew through the straps to fly away, detonating the bomb. The bomb would flare for eight minutes with a twenty-two-inch flame. The Pentagon planned to use these bat bombs to set fire to Japan's rickety wood houses and buildings.

After researching Project X-Ray for two years and recruiting two million bats from the American Southwest, the army tested the bat bombs in New Mexico. During the testing, several bats escaped, setting fire to a large aircraft hangar and a general's staff car. The navy took over the project and decided to freeze the bats into hibernation before dropping them out of the bombers. In a test run in August 1944, the frozen bats were dropped out of the bombers, remained asleep, and penetrated into the earth. Project X-Ray was suspended, having cost American taxpayers $2 million.

You've Got the Wrong Man

In 1994, the United States Postal Service printed a special stamp series called Legends of the West, including a stamp of African-American cowboy and rodeo star Bill Pickett. When Pickett's descendants informed the Postal Service that the stamp portrayed not Bill, but his brother Ben, the Postal Service recalled the stamps from every post office—at a cost of $1.1 million.

The Needless Battle

The War of 1812 ended with the signing of the Treaty of Ghent in Belgium on December 24, 1814. News traveled slowly to America, and British major general Sir Edward Pakenham, unaware that the war had ended, sent more than eight thousand troops to capture New Orleans. On January 8, 1815, fifteen days after the war had ended, General Andrew Jackson led his troops to victory against the British in the Battle of New Orleans, also known as "the needless battle," killing approximately 1,500 British soldiers, including Sir Edward Pakenham, and losing seventy-one American troops.

So Much for Lady Luck

In 1994, the Beardstown Ladies, a group of fourteen grandmothers who had started an investment club in 1983 in Beardstown, Illinois, claimed a 23.4 percent annualized ten-year return to publicize their book, *The Beardstown Ladies' Common-Sense Investment Guide.* The book spent three weeks on the best-seller list, leading to four more books and dozens of national television appearances.

In 1998, when *Chicago* magazine challenged the Beardstown Ladies' 23.4 percent claim, the ladies hired Price Waterhouse to audit their books, only to discover that they had bungled their figures. Their actual return was 9.1 percent annualized over that same ten-year period—far less than the Standard & Poor's 500 average annual return of 14.9 percent or the average general-stock-fund return of 12.6 percent during that same period. The little old ladies turned out to be little old frauds.

One Bad Apple

Between 1978 and 1982, Beech-Nut executives—determined to save the company an estimated $250,000 a year and boost profits—arranged for all Beech-Nut bottles labeled "100 percent" pure apple juice, consumed by babies, to be filled with a mixture of water and a bogus apple juice concentrate made solely from sugar and flavorings. After a trade association exposed this abhorrent fraud, the United States government fined Beech-Nut $2 million for 215 violations of the Federal Food, Drug, and Cosmetic Act. A criminal court sentenced former Beech-Nut president Niels Hoyvald and vice president John Lavery to jail for one year and fined each executive $100,000.

Catastrophe

During the Middle Ages, Europeans considered cats evil and associated them with witchcraft and the devil. They killed hundreds of thousands of cats, which likely led to the huge increase in the rat population in Europe and the resulting spread of bubonic plague that killed a quarter of the European people in the fourteenth century.

Bellyaches

In November 1974, plastic surgeon Howard Bellin performed a tummy tuck on Virginia O'Hare of Poughkeepsie, New York, and accidentally moved her belly button two inches off center and left her with a thick twenty-inch scar across her midsection. O'Hare sued for malpractice and in 1979 won an $854,000 judgment against the doctor.

An Eerie Resemblance

When low-budget film director Edward D. Wood Jr. made his 1959 science fiction movie, *Plan 9 from Outer Space*, he salvaged five minutes of silent film footage he had previously shot of recently deceased actor Bela Lugosi for another movie and hired his wife's chiropractor, Tom Mason, as a stand-in for Lugosi, despite the fact that Mason looked nothing like the actor and was noticeably taller. Wood directed the miscast chiropractor to hunch over and hold a cape over his face throughout the film, which was billed as Lugosi's last movie. In 1980, film critic Michael Medved dubbed *Plan 9 from Outer Space* "the worst movie ever made."

Toast of the Town

In 1926, Charles Strite, inventor of the world's first pop-up toaster, introduced the Toastmaster, the first pop-up toaster that would allow families to make perfect toast in the comfort of their homes—complete with a dial to adjust the desired degree of darkness. Unfortunately, the Toastmaster grew hotter after making each slice of toast. The first slice popped up underdone, and the sixth slice popped up burned to a crisp.

Anaximenes the Airhead

The sixth-century Greek philosopher Anaximenes of Miletus believed that air was the basic substance of the universe, and everything else—stars, planets, oceans, plants, animals—came from air through rarefaction or condensation.

Copycat

On August 23, 1987, Delaware senator Joe Biden, running for the Democratic nomination for president, delivered a speech at the Iowa State Fair in which he plagiarized a section of a speech given in May 1987 by Neil Kinnock, British Labour Party candidate for prime minister. When the press reported the similarity between the speeches and then discovered that Biden had been accused of plagiarism as a first-year law student at Syracuse University, Biden dropped out of the presidential race.

Bible Blunders

Snug As a Bug

A 1551 version of the Bible mistranslated the verse "Thou shalt not be afraid for the terror by night" (Psalm 91:5) as "Thou shalt not be afraid of any buggies at night."

Breeches in Eden

A 1560 version of the Bible, published in Geneva, translated Genesis 3:7 to read that Adam and Eve "sewed fig leaves together and made themselves breeches." Breeches are knee-length trousers that did not exist in biblical times.

What? No Neosporin?

A 1568 version of the Bishop's Bible mistranslated the line "Is there no balm in Gilead?" from Jeremiah 8:22 as "Is there no treacle in Gilead?" Treacle, a medicinal compound once used as an antidote against venom, did not exist during biblical times.

Fools Rush In

A 1763 version of the Bible printed in England accidentally substituted the word *a* for *no* so that Psalm 14:1 reads, "The fool hath said in his heart there is a God." The printer was fined £3,000 and every available copy was destroyed.

Bad Advice

In 1716, the first Bible printed in Ireland included a typographical error that changed the line "Go and sin no more" in John 5:14 to "Go and sin on more."

Bathroom Reading

The Living Bible published in 1971 in the United States modernized I Samuel 24:3 from "And Saul went in to cover his feet" to "Saul went into a cave to go to the bathroom."

If the Shoe Fits

A version of the Bible in an Eskimo dialect included one misplaced letter so that the verse "nation shall rise up against nation" (Mark 13:8) became "a pair of snowshoes shall rise up against a pair of snowshoes."

Bad Blood

The ancient Greek physician Galen (circa 130–200 CE), considered the father of experimental physiology, mistakenly believed that the body is governed by four humors (blood, phlegm, black bile, and yellow bile) and that a disorder of any one of the four humors causes disease. He incorrectly claimed that a doctor could cure diseases by bleeding the patient to remove the "corrupt humors." If a patient did not recover from a disease after a pint of blood was removed from the body, the physician would remove more blood—weakening the patient further and often hastening death. Galen's absurd remedy was widely practiced by physicians and barbers for the next 1,500 years, resulting in the deaths of millions of people, including British poet Lord Byron and England's King Charles II.

The Seeds of Destruction

In 1876, Brazilian customs officials allowed English botanist Sir Henry Wickham to take seventy thousand rubber tree seeds from Brazil to England. Wickham insisted the seeds were botanical specimens to be used solely for the royal plant collection at Kew Gardens. He germinated the seedlings at Kew Gardens and then sent them to Ceylon and Malaya, breaking the Brazilian monopoly on raw rubber and causing the collapse of the Brazilian rubber industry.

The Kiss of Death

In 1592, the Inquisition arrested Italian scientist and philosopher Giordano Bruno (1548–1600), jailing him for seven years as he stood trial for heresy for insisting that the earth is round, the universe is infinite, life exists on other planets, the sun does not revolve around the earth, and the earth is not the center of the universe. In 1600, Pope Clement VIII sentenced Giordano Bruno to be burned alive at the stake.

The Miracle of the Hubcaps

In the 1968 movie *Bullitt*, Steve McQueen's Dodge Charger loses three hubcaps during the long car chase scene, but when he crashes the car at the end of the chase, three more hubcaps somehow fly off the car.

Read My Lips

In his acceptance speech at the Republican National Convention on August 18, 1988, presidential candidate George Bush firmly stated, "Read my lips: No new taxes." In 1990, as president of the United States, Bush raised taxes, enabling Democratic presidential candidate Bill Clinton to use Bush's words against him in a television commercial during the 1992 presidential campaign.

The Whole Ball of Wax

In October 2009, Louis Tussaud's Waxworks advertised the grand opening of its wax museum in Thailand by posting a billboard along a prominent highway of mass murderer Adolf Hitler giving a Nazi salute above a slogan in Thai that read: "Hitler is not dead." After receiving complaints from the German and Israeli embassies, the museum covered up the billboard. "We didn't choose Hitler with the intention of praising him," said museum director Somporn Naksuetrong, "but because he is well known."

Son of a Gun

In the last shootout in the 1969 western movie *Butch Cassidy and the Sundance Kid*, actor Robert Redford fires seventeen shots from two six-shooters—without reloading his guns.

Biting the Hand That Feeds It

In 1996, Mattel introduced the Cabbage Patch Snacktime Kids doll, which had a motorized jaw that enabled it to mimic eating plastic cookies and other foods. Parents reported that the doll also ate children's hair and fingers. Mattel first tried putting warning labels on the dolls but ultimately recalled the dolls and offered each consumer a $40 refund.

Out of Order

Around 738 BCE, Romulus, the first emperor of Rome, instituted a calendar that contained only 304 days, for a total of ten months: Marius, Aprilis, Maius, Junius, Quitilis, Sextilis, September, October, November, and December. The prefixes of the last six months were taken from the Roman words for "five," "six," "seven," "eight," "nine," and "ten." The second Roman emperor, Numa Pompilius, added two more months to the calendar (January at the beginning of the calendar and February at the end of the calendar). In 452 BCE, the decemvirs changed the order of the months, putting January first and February second. In 46 BCE, Roman emperor Julius Caesar moved New Year's Day from March 1 to January 1. Centuries later the Romans changed the name of the month of Quitilis to July (in memory of Julius Caesar) and the name of Sextilis to August (in memory of Caesar Augustus). To this day, September (with the Roman prefix for "seven") is the ninth month of the calendar, October (with the prefix for "eight") is the tenth month, November (with the prefix for "nine") is the eleventh month, and December (with the prefix for "ten") is the twelfth month.

Heartless Cardiology

While working at Harvard and Emory universities in the 1970s and early 1980s, cardiology researcher John R. Darsee wrote more than one hundred papers, published in the esteemed *New England Journal of Medicine*, *Proceedings of the National Academy of Sciences*, and *The American Journal of Cardiology*. How did he do it? In 1981, investigators at the National Institutes of Health discovered that Darsee had fabricated much of the data cited in those papers.

Capitol Offense

In 1791, architect Pierre L'Enfant designed the Capitol building in Washington, D.C., to face east, expecting the city to grow toward the Anacostia Harbor. The city developed toward the west, leaving the Capitol with its back to the city.

Clone Dethroned

In 2004, South Korean scientist Dr. Woo Suk Hwang, a professor of veterinary medicine at Seoul National University, announced that he had cloned human embryos and extracted stem cells from them, prompting *Time* magazine to name him one of the world's one hundred most influential people and the South Korean government to promote him as a candidate for a Nobel Prize. A 2005 investigation at Seoul National University revealed that Hwang had fabricated the results of his research and embezzled $3 billion in government research funds.

Captain Kidd's Kinky Cat

A printer's error caused the 1991 edition of the 1956 children's book *Captain Kidd's Cat*, by Robert Lawson, to include a thirty-two-page section from the sexually explicit 1989 novel *Closer*, by Dennis Cooper, which concerns sadomasochistic homosexual relationships.

Securities and Exchange Omission

On November 7, 2005, Boston derivatives expert Harry Markopolos submitted a twenty-one-page memo to the Securities and Exchange Commission (SEC) titled "The World's Largest Hedge Fund Is a Fraud," alleging that hedge fund investor Bernie Madoff was operating a Ponzi scheme. Markopolos identified twenty red flags showing that Madoff's steady returns were not possible. The SEC ignored Markopolos's detailed memo and follow-up reports. Three years later, on December 11, 2008, Bernie Madoff freely admitted the fraud to his two sons, who promptly reported him to investigators, and the FBI arrested Madoff for bilking $50 billion from school endowments, pension funds, and retirement accounts. In the subsequent months, investigators discovered that the SEC had botched six investigations of Madoff since 1992.

Blowing It

In his nomination acceptance speech at the Democratic National Convention on August 14, 1980, President Jimmy Carter accidentally referred to former Vice President Hubert Horatio Humphrey, renowned for his loquaciousness, as "Hubert Horatio Hornblower." Captain Horatio Hornblower is the reluctant hero in a series of novels by C. S. Forester about the British Royal Navy in the days of sailing ships.

Wipe Out

On December 19, 1973, *The Tonight Show* host Johnny Carson joked in his monologue: "You know what else is disappearing from the supermarkets' shelves? Toilet paper. There's an acute shortage of toilet paper in the United States." In response, Americans began hoarding toilet paper, creating a three-week toilet paper shortage in the United States.

True to His Name

In May 1985, colleagues at the University of California, San Diego School of Medicine began questioning how cardiologist Robert Slutsky churned out a new research paper roughly every ten days, while other researchers in his field produced a new paper once every few months. Slutsky responded by resigning from his position and moving to New York. University investigators concluded that Slutsky had produced thirteen fraudulent papers by altering data, lying about his research methods, listing coauthors who had not been involved in the research, recycling data from earlier research, avoiding peer reviews of his data and manuscripts, and forging other researchers' signatures.

Isn't That Special?

In March 1998, cardiac surgeon Elias Hanna performed a double bypass operation on former *Saturday Night Live* cast member Dana Carvey and bypassed the wrong artery, leaving the damaged section untouched and the heart vulnerable to an attack. Carvey—best known for his portrayals of the Church Lady, Hans the Bodybuilder, George Bush, and Garth Algar (featured in the *Wayne's World* films with Mike Myers)—sued the surgeon for $7.5 million, settled out of court, and donated the money to charity.

Refusing to Give an Inch

In May 1977, philanthropists Edith and Henry Everett withdrew their $3-million donation to rebuild the Children's Zoo in New York's Central Park because the New York City Art Commission refused to spell out their names in letters more than two inches tall on a commemorative plaque. Ultimately, the Tisch Foundation, headed by Laurence and Preston Robert Tisch, donated $4.5 million to rebuild the Children's Zoo, without any requirements about their names on a plaque.

Full Blast Ahead

NASA engineers had warned that the $900 synthetic rubber O-ring seal on the space shuttle *Challenger*'s solid rocket fuel booster, made by the Morton Thiokol aerospace company, was vulnerable at temperatures below 51 degrees Fahrenheit. Despite these warnings, NASA launched the $1.2 billion *Challenger* on January 28, 1986, in 36-degree weather. Seventy-three seconds after liftoff, the *Challenger* exploded, killing the seven astronauts aboard and ending further shuttle flights for nearly three years.

Kick the Habit

For the 1969 movie *Change of Habit*, producers miscast rock 'n' roll legend Elvis Presley to star as a doctor who runs a health clinic in an inner-city neighborhood and wins the confidence of his patients by singing bubble-gum music, aided by actress Mary Tyler Moore, miscast as a nun.

Thinking with His Chappaquiddick

Around eleven p.m. on July 18, 1969, Massachusetts senator Ted Kennedy left a party on Chappaquiddick Island (off Martha's Vineyard) with his brother Bobby's former secretary, Mary Jo Kopechne, and accidentally drove off the Dike Bridge. He swam from the submerged upside-down car and fled the scene of the accident, leaving Kopechne in the sunken vehicle. Nearly ten hours later, at 9:45 a.m., Kennedy arrived at the Edgartown police station to report the accident. He told Chief Dominick Arena that he had made a wrong turn at 11:15 p.m. on the way to the ferry landing on Chappaquiddick, driven off the Dike Bridge, returned to his hotel room, and fallen asleep. He decided to contact the police when he "fully realized" what had happened. Police divers found the dead body of Kopechne in the submerged car. On July 25, Kennedy pleaded guilty and was given a two-month suspended sentence and one year of probation by Edgartown District Court judge James A. Boyle.

Speculation that Kennedy, a married man, had drunkenly driven off the bridge on his way to the beach for a tryst with Kopechne and then waited until he sobered up to report the accident to authorities ruined any hope Kennedy had to wage a successful bid for the presidency of the United States in 1972. Kennedy's presidential bid in 1980 was similarly dogged by unanswered questions about the Chappaquiddick incident.

Baywatch Gets Beached

In 1990, NBC canceled the television action drama *Baywatch* after just one season on the air. Spurred by the show's loyal following, lead actor David Hasselhoff invested his own money to revive the series for first-run syndication on the USA network starting in September 1991. *Baywatch* ran for the next ten years and was, according to *The Guinness Book of World Records*, the most widely viewed television series in the world ever, with an estimated weekly audience of more than 1.1 billion viewers worldwide in 1996.

Charge of the Light Brigade

On October 25, 1854, during the Crimean War, the Russians retreated from the port city of Balaklava, taking captured Turkish artillery with them. Seeing this, Lord Raglan, commander of the opposing British troops, sent one of his men, Captain Louis Edward Nolan, to order the British brigade of light cavalry, commanded by Lord Cardigan, to stop the Russians from taking the Turkish cannons. Nolan miscommunicated the order, directing the light brigade to prevent the Russians from taking *any* cannons—Turkish or Russian. The resulting charge by the 673 men of the light brigade left 113 British soldiers dead and another 134 wounded or captured. English poet Lord Tennyson glorified the courage of the British troops in his poem "The Charge of the Light Brigade" with the frequently quoted line: "Theirs not to reason why, / Theirs but to do and die."

Wholly Cow

Scientists at the Institute for Animal Health in Edinburgh, Scotland, working under a £217,000 government grant to determine whether the nation's sheep were infected with bovine spongiform encephalopathy (better known as mad cow disease), discovered in 2001 that they had spent four years testing cattle brains instead of sheep brains. Two independent investigations revealed that the cow brains and sheep brains, leftover from two previous experiments, had been labeled improperly and stored in the same freezer, where they accidentally got mixed together.

Blast from the Past

On April 25, 1986, Soviet authorities at the Chernobyl nuclear power station in the Ukraine at Pripyat (ten miles from Chernobyl and sixty-five miles from Kiev) ran a test on Reactor 4 to find out how long the turbines would continue generating power after the reactor was switched off. The technicians shut down the emergency water-cooling system, the emergency shutdown system, and the power-regulating system, and withdrew nearly all the rods from the reactor core. When they shut off the steam supply to the turbines, the pumps circulating water to cool the reactor core slowed down, causing the temperature of the core to rise abruptly. With all the safety systems shut off, the reactor overheated, prompting a chain reaction in the core that caused a massive explosion at 1:23 a.m. on April 26, blowing the steel and concrete lid off the reactor and the roof off the building, releasing one hundred times more radiation than the Hiroshima and Nagasaki bombs combined.

In Space, No One Can Hear You Scream

In most science fiction movies, the rockets on spacecraft make a violent roaring sound and explosions as they travel through space. In reality, spacecrafts do not make any sounds in space, since space is a vacuum.

Gingerly

In the late nineteenth century, Andrew Smith, whose bearded face is depicted on boxes of Smith Brothers Cough Drops to this very day, refused to allow ginger ale in his house because, as a fervent prohibitionist, he objected to the alcoholic nature of its name. Ginger ale does not contain any alcohol.

Give 'Em Hell, Harry

On November 3, 1948, the headline on the front page of an edition of the *Chicago Daily Tribune* declared "Dewey Defeats Truman." President Harry Truman actually won that election, winning 303 electoral votes, while New York governor Thomas E. Dewey received only 189.

Not Your Cup of Tea

When tea was first introduced in the American colonies, many housewives, in their ignorance, served the tea leaves with sugar or syrup after throwing away the water in which they had been boiled.

What a Rush

On October 10, 1993, conservative talk show host Rush Limbaugh admitted that he was addicted to prescription pain medication as a result of spinal surgery and checked himself into a rehabilitation program for thirty days. Limbaugh's housekeeper, Wilma Cline, had told the *National Enquirer* and authorities in Palm Beach, Florida, that she had helped Limbaugh illegally hoard thousands of prescription painkillers and that he took as many as thirty OxyContin pills a day. Two year later, on October 5, 1995, Limbaugh told viewers of his short-lived television show, "If people are violating the law by doing drugs, they ought to be accused and they ought to be convicted and they ought to be sent up." On April 28, 2006, after a three-year investigation, police arrested Limbaugh and charged him with fraud for illegally deceiving four doctors in six months in order to receive overlapping prescriptions at a pharmacy. Despite Limbaugh's previous pronouncements that drug crimes deserve punishment, prosecutors agreed to drop the charge without a guilty plea if Limbaugh continued treatment.

Plane Stupid

In the 1970s, the People's Republic of China, having bought ten Boeing 707s and forty Pratt & Whitney replacement engines, ordered its aeronautical engineers to secretly build a copy of the Boeing 707 to be powered by one of the replacement engines. The plane, called the Y-10, could not fly. Chinese engineers had accidentally mislocated the plane's center of gravity.

Do Your Homework

On November 2, 1999, Andy Hiller, the political correspondent for WHDH-TV, in Boston, asked presidential candidate George W.

Bush to name the leaders of Chechnya, Pakistan, India, and Taiwan. Bush could only identify the president of Taiwan as "Lee," then retorted, "Can you name the foreign minister of Mexico?" Hiller replied that he was not the one running for president. After the interview, Bush spokesperson Karen Hughes attempted to defend Bush by foolishly admitting that neither Bush's senior foreign policy adviser Josh Bolten nor his foreign policy adviser Joel Shinn could name all four of these world leaders.

A Fine Kettle of Fish

In 1982, *People* magazine referred to actor Abe Vigoda, who portrayed Detective Fish on the television sitcom *Barney Miller*, as "the late Abe Vigoda." Still alive and well, Vigoda posed for a photograph showing him sitting up in a coffin, holding a copy of the erroneous magazine article.

Shifting Gears

In the fall of 1975, the Chrysler Corporation, determined to boost quarterly sales figures by selling small cars that felt like big cars, introduced the 1976 Dodge Aspen and its sister car, the 1976 Plymouth Volare, with great fanfare, rushing the cars to market. Within the next two years, Chrysler recalled more than 3.5 million Aspens and Volares and spent more than $200 million on repairs.

Fuzzy Math

When the Romans captured the city of Syracuse on the island of Sicily in 212 BCE, the Roman commander, Marcellus, ordered his soldiers not to harm the Greek mathematician Archimedes, who lived in the city. The Roman soldiers, however, failed to recognize Archimedes and killed him.

Stung by Stingers

In 1986, to combat the Soviet invasion of Afghanistan, the CIA gave approximately one thousand shoulder-launched Stinger missiles, purchased by the U.S. government from General Dynamics for $35,000 each, to the Afghan rebels for free. After the Russians withdrew from Afghanistan in 1989, the Afghans sold some of the Stingers to Iran and North Korea, demanding $100,000 apiece for the weapons. Peeved, Congress budgeted more than $65 million for the CIA to buy back remaining Stingers from the Afghans.

Loose Cannon

On August 12, 1861, Confederate troops fired on Fort Sumter, in South Carolina, beginning the first battle of the Civil War. Although the battle lasted for thirty-four hours, no one was killed. Two days later, on August 14, while Union soldiers, preparing to abandon the fort, fired a salute to the flag, a cannon discharged prematurely, accidentally killing Private Daniel Hough—the first casualty of the Civil War.

Misty Translation

Clairol introduced its Mist Stick curling iron in Germany only to discover that in German the word *mist* is slang for "manure."

Spell It Out

In 1796, a city in Ohio was named after its founder, Moses Cleaveland, a surveyor for the Connecticut Land Company. In 1831, the city's first newspaper, the *Cleveland Advertiser*, misspelled the city's name on its masthead as Cleveland. The city's name has been incorrectly spelled Cleveland ever since.

Put That in Your Pipe and Smoke It

On March 29, 1992, Democratic presidential candidate Bill Clinton, responding to a question at a candidates' forum on WCBS-TV, in New York, admitted that he had smoked marijuana while attending Oxford University as a Rhodes Scholar between 1968 and 1970. "I've never broken a state law," he said. "But when I was in England I experimented with marijuana a time or two, and I didn't like it. I didn't inhale it, and never tried it again." If he didn't inhale, asked critics, how did he know he didn't like it?

Happiness in the Mouth

When the Coca-Cola Company introduced Coke in China in 1982, Chinese shopkeepers transliterated the brand name Coca-Cola as Kekoukela, without any regard for the actual meaning of the sounds in Chinese. In different dialects, *kekoukela* translates as "bite the wax tadpole" or "female horse stuffed with wax." The Coca-Cola Company researched forty thousand characters to find the phonetic equivalent *kokou kole*, which translates to "happiness in the mouth."

No Contest

In March 1982, a Coca-Cola bottler in Cookeville, Tennessee, launched a contest in which players would win $2,000 if they collected bottle caps embossed with individual letters of the alphabet to spell out "home run." The bottler ordered just a few bottle caps printed with the letter *R* so that the chances of winning the contest would be a million to one. When huge numbers of winners began turning up, the bottler discovered that the printer had made eighteen thousand caps embossed with the letter *R*—costing the bottler more than $100,000 in prize awards before the bottler backed out of the contest.

Cold Fusion Delusion

On March 23, 1989, chemistry professors Martin Fleischmann of the University of Southampton and B. Stanley Pons of the University of Utah announced that they had achieved nuclear fusion at normal room temperature in a jar of water. The chemists claimed that they had used electrodes made of palladium and platinum to electrolyze deuterium, causing a neutron to fuse with a proton, releasing energy. The Utah legislature immediately allocated $5 million for the University of Utah to set up the National Cold Fusion Institute. In November 1989, Fleischmann and Pons mysteriously disappeared the night before a critical University review, and the United States Department of Energy reported that the evidence for cold fusion "was not persuasive." The National Cold Fusion Institute closed in 1991.

A Kick in the Teeth

Colgate-Palmolive introduced a toothpaste in France called Cue, unaware that *Cue* is the name of a notorious French pornography magazine.

Dazed and Confused

In the fifteenth century, Italian explorer Christopher Columbus miscalculated the circumference of the globe by 7,600 miles, inaccurately estimating the earth to be 25 percent smaller than it actually is. Determined to sail from Europe across the Atlantic Ocean to Asia, he failed to predict the existence of a landmass between the two continents, and after four trips he remained convinced he had landed in Asia—not the New World. Unbeknownst to Columbus, he actually discovered the Bahamian island of San Salvador (which he believed to be an island of the Indies), Cuba (which he thought to be a part of China), and the Dominican Republic (which he insisted was the Far East). He named the islands the West Indies (because he incorrectly thought they were part of the Indies islands of Asia) and dubbed the natives Indians (wrongly convinced he was in India). Columbus also claimed that the delta of the Orinoco River, near present-day Trinidad and Tobago, was the entrance to the Garden of Eden.

All That Glitters Is Not Gold

In 1522, Spanish conquistador Gil Gonzáles Dávila gave the country Costa Rica its name (meaning "rich coast") because he saw natives wearing gold necklaces and jumped to the conclusion that the land was rich with gold. The Spanish never found much gold or minerals in Costa Rica. In fact, Costa Rica has less gold than any country in Latin America.

Stupendous Comet Fizzles Out

On March 7, 1973, Czech astronomer Luboš Kohoutek sighted a comet streaking toward the sun. Several prominent scientists predicted that in January 1974 the comet, named Kohoutek, with a tail fifty million miles long, would light up the sky, glowing brighter than the moon. The comet actually appeared as nothing more than a faint streak of light in the sky near Venus and Jupiter.

Ho Ho Ho!

In the 1960s, Pillsbury marketed its Jolly Green Giant products in Saudi Arabia. Unfortunately, *Jolly Green Giant* was translated literally into Arabic as "Intimidating Green Ogre."

The $12-Million Delegate

In 1980, former Texas governor John B. Connally, having spent fourteen months and $12 million of his own money running for the Republican presidential nomination, won only one delegate to the Republican Convention: Mrs. Ada Mills of Clarksville, Arkansas.

A Sad State of Affairs

In the U.S. Senate election held on November 2, 1962, approximately 46,000 Connecticut voters wrote in Edward M. Kennedy on their ballots for senator. Kennedy was running for senator in Massachusetts, not Connecticut.

A Real Bomb

In the 1956 movie *The Conqueror*, RKO producer-director Dick Powell cast John Wayne to star as Mongolian warrior Genghis Khan, which the *Los Angeles Times* described as history's "most improbable piece of casting unless Mickey Rooney were to play Jesus in *King of Kings*." Powell filmed the movie at Snow Canyon in Utah, a radioactive dust trap 137 miles from the army's atomic bomb test site at Yucca Flat. By 1986, ninety-one of the 220 members of the cast and crew who had worked on location on the film had developed cancer. Forty-six of those people had died from it, including John Wayne, his costar Susan Hayward, and Powell.

Bad for Constitution

The Founding Fathers neglected to put any provisions in the Constitution to replace the president in case the chief executive died or was removed from office by impeachment or disability. The Constitution states only that the "powers and duties" of the president "shall devolve on the Vice-President." When President William Henry Harrison died in 1841, Vice President John Tyler assumed the powers and duties of the president legally, but referred to himself as the president of the United States illegally, setting a precedent for other vice presidents to follow suit. In 1967, Congress approved the Twenty-fifth Amendment to correct the oversight, stating that if the president is temporarily disabled, the vice president serves as acting president, and if the president dies, resigns, or is removed from office, the vice president becomes president.

Breaking Loose

In the 1980s, when the advertising agency working for Adolph Coors Company translated the Coors Light slogan "Turn It Loose" into Spanish for the American Hispanic market, the copywriter accidentally altered the meaning of the words to "Suffer from Diarrhea."

Kellogg's Gets Flaky

In 1964, the Kellogg Company and the Post Cereal Company, eager to cash in on the concept of freeze-dried food popularized by the space program, added freeze-dried fruit to their Corn Flakes cereals. Consumers quickly discovered that the pieces of freeze-dried fruit in the Corn Flakes had to soak in milk for nearly ten minutes before they become reconstituted, by which time the Corn Flakes were soggy and unappetizing.

Montezuma's Mistake

In 1519, Aztec emperor Montezuma welcomed bearded Spanish conquistador Hernando Cortés to Mexico, convinced he was the exiled, fair-skinned, bearded wind god Quetzalcoatl, whose imminent return had been predicted by some Aztec priests. Cortés soon imprisoned Montezuma, ruling the Aztec empire through him, seizing massive amounts of gold, and ruthlessly destroying Aztec temples.

Two-Way Street

In the late 1950s, geneticist Francis Crick, who discovered the double helix structure of DNA with James Watson, insisted that DNA makes RNA, but not vice versa. He was wrong. In 1983, Pasteur Institute researcher Françoise Barré-Sinoussi discovered that the genetic material of the HIV virus is RNA, which makes DNA.

A Diseased Mind

In 1658, Puritan leader Oliver Cromwell, suffering from malaria, refused to take the cure—the bark of the cinchona tree—because he wrongly believed the bark remedy to be part of a Catholic plot to poison non-Catholics. Cromwell died of malaria.

Oh, What a Tangled Web We Weave

In 1994, Arkansas state employee Paula Corbin Jones filed a sexual harassment lawsuit against President Bill Clinton, alleging that while governor of Arkansas in 1991, he summoned her to a Little Rock hotel room, exposed himself, and made an unwanted sexual advance. Clinton refused to settle the case, and Jones's lawyers, seeking to establish a pattern of Clinton's sexual misconduct, discovered his relationship with White House intern Monica Lewinsky—which ultimately resulted in impeachment proceedings against Clinton in 1998. On November 13, 1998, Clinton settled with Jones, agreeing to pay her $850,000, but with no apology or admission of guilt. Had Clinton settled the lawsuit in 1994, he would have likely avoided the impeachment proceedings.

Time Out

In the 1935 movie *The Crusades*, directed by Cecil B. DeMille and taking place between 1189 and 1199, King Richard the Lion-Hearted flips back his cloak to check his watch. Watches were not invented until at least the 1400s, and wristwatches did not become popular for men until the 1900s.

The Misdiagnosed Poster Child

In 1975, the Cystic Fibrosis Foundation chose six-year-old Rodney Brown as its poster child. Brown, examined at fifteen months of age by an Indiana doctor and diagnosed with the respiratory disease cystic fibrosis, had received treatment for five years. In 1980, doctors at Johns Hopkins tested Brown and discovered that he never had cystic fibrosis. He had asthma.

Get the Picture?

On June 6, 1944, *Life* magazine photographer Robert Capa went ashore with E Company to Omaha Beach in the first wave on D-Day and shot three thirty-six-exposure rolls of film. He swiftly returned to a landing craft, which brought him back unharmed to a ship. Upon his return to England, his unprocessed film was flown to New York for developing and printing. The lab technician set the film-drying cabinet on high, inadvertently melting the negatives. Only eleven photographs survived—and those were blurred.

Milking It

When the National Dairy Council expanded its "Got Milk?" advertising campaign for the Hispanic market, promoters translated the slogan as "¿Tienes leche?" which literally means "Are you lactating?"

Coffee Mach Frei

In January 2009, the German coffee company Tchibo and the gas station chain Esso ran a joint advertising campaign using the slogan *"Jedem den Seinen,"* which can be translated as "to each his own" or "to each what he deserves." The identical words hung over the entrance to Buchenwald, a Nazi concentration camp near the city of Weimar. Public outrage compelled the companies to discontinue the advertising campaign.

Spelling Trouble

The Art of Misspelling

In 2004, artist Maria Alquilar constructed a $40,000 ceramic mural at a new city library in Livermore, California, misspelling the names of Albert Einstein, William Shakespeare, Vincent van Gogh, Michelangelo, and seven other historical figures. Alquilar begrudgingly fixed the names but refused to apologize, insisting that artistic license gave her the right to spell the names any way she wished.

Sex Education

On September 16, 2010, the city of South Bend, Indiana, erected a digital billboard that urged passersby to visit a Web site where they could read the "15 best things about our pubic schools."

Back to School

On August 6, 2010, road painters hired to paint the word *school* across freshly repaved Drake Road outside Southern Guilford High School in North Carolina designated the area a "shcool" zone.

A Freudian Typo

On August 19, 2008, a news article dispatched from the Associated Press described Senator Joseph Lieberman as a former "Democratic vice-presidential prick."

I Have a Dictionary

On January 15, 2007, KIII-TV in Corpus Christi, Texas, aired a news report showing local community members honoring the memory of Dr. Martin Luther King by carrying signs printed with the misspelled slogans "I Have a Draem" and "I Have a Deram."

A Bright Future for Proofreaders

On May 31, 2007, Democratic presidential candidate Hillary Clinton pitched a technology plan to Silicon Valley executives in Santa Clara, California, standing at a podium in front of a blue banner emblazoned with the misspelled message "New Jobs for Tommorrow" in large white letters.

Giving Themselves a Bad Name

On July 21, 2008, the New Hampshire–based *Valley News* misspelled its own name across the front-page banner as *Valley Newss*.

On the Ball

In April 2009, two prominent baseball players on the Washington Nationals took to the field wearing jerseys emblazoned with the team's name misspelled as "Natinals."

Ka-Boom!

On September 18, 1980, an air force repairman accidentally dropped a wrench socket, which fell eighty feet into a missile silo near Damascus, Arkansas, hitting a Titan II ICBM missile and causing a leak in a pressurized fuel tank. Authorities evacuated the base and surrounding area, and eight hours later, fuel vapors ignited and exploded, catapulting the nuclear warhead six hundred feet, killing one man and injuring eleven others.

A Nose for Business

In 1973, former General Motors executive John DeLorean, creator of the Pontiac GTO, left his $650,000-salary job, raised some $175 million in financing, and in 1974 formed the DeLorean Motor Company, building his car factory in Northern Ireland. In 1982, DeLorean was videotaped in a government sting operation attempting to broker a $24-million cocaine deal to rescue his financially troubled company.

Dream As If You'll Live Forever

In September 1955, actor James Dean filmed a thirty-second public service commercial for the National Highway Safety Committee, ad-libbing, "Take it easy driving. The life you save may be mine." Two weeks later, he was killed while speeding in his Porsche.

Life, Liberty, and the
Pursuit of Slavery

In June 1776, after Thomas Jefferson drafted the Declaration of
Independence, Benjamin Franklin and John Adams made a few
minor literary changes. Congress, however, deleted several passages from the draft, including a grievance against King George for
supporting slavery: "He has waged cruel war against human nature
itself, violating its most sacred rights of life & liberty in the persons
of a distant people who never offended him, captivating & carrying
them into slavery in another hemisphere, or to incur miserable
death in their transportation thither." Had this passage remained
in the Declaration of Independence, the United States might have
outlawed slavery and emancipated the slaves at the onset, averting
the Civil War.

The Psychic Spy Network

In 1995, the U.S. Defense Intelligence Agency admitted having
spent $20 million over the previous seventeen years on psychics,
without achieving any significant results. The agency had sought
the help of psychics in failed attempts to locate Scud missile launchers being moved around the desert by Saddam Hussein during
Operation Desert Storm, to find Americans taken hostage, and to
thwart a perceived threat from terrorist Carlos the Jackal.

The Big Boob

On January 28, 2002, United States Attorney General John Ashcroft announced that he had spent $8,000 of the taxpayers' money for drapes to veil the exposed breast of *Spirit of Justice*, an eighteen-foot-tall aluminum statue of a woman that stands in the Great Hall of the Department of Justice in Washington, D.C. Ashcroft insisted that he had ordered the drapes so that a large breast would not appear behind him during press conferences. Critics insisted that despite the draped statue, photographers and television cameras would still be focused on a big boob.

Sour Atoms

The Greek natural philosopher Democritus (circa 470–380 BCE) first proposed the theory that all matter is composed of atoms. However, he also incorrectly theorized that atoms are solid and cannot be split, that sharp atoms cause sour tastes, and that the human soul is made up of the smallest atoms in the universe.

Driving to Distraction

In 1977, American car manufacturers made 9.3 million cars. That same year, American car manufacturers recalled 10.4 million cars.

Quixotic and Idiotic

In the seventeenth century novel *Don Quixote*, by Miguel de Cervantes, peasant laborer Sancho Panza sells his donkey, and then, without any explanation, is depicted riding it again. He loses his coat with food in the pocket, but later, inexplicably, possesses the food. His helmet is shattered into pieces, but later, the headgear mysteriously reappears intact and unscathed.

East Meets West

In the 1944 movie *Dragon Seed*, based on the novel by Pearl S. Buck, Academy Award–winning actress Katharine Hepburn, absurdly miscast as a Chinese peasant named Jade, speaks with a cultured Connecticut accent.

A Flighty Candidate

During his 1996 campaign for senator, Louisiana Republican candidate David Duke, having insisted that his previous activities as a grand wizard of the Ku Klux Klan and an advocate of Nazism were "youthful indiscretions," claimed that recent TWA and Valujet airplane crashes had been the result of "affirmative action programs."

Shock Treatment

In 1972, Democratic presidential candidate George McGovern chose Missouri senator Thomas Eagleton to be his vice presidential candidate. Twelve days later, Eagleton revealed that he had been hospitalized three times between 1960 and 1966 for mental illness, twice receiving electric-shock therapy for depression. McGovern insisted that he backed Eagleton "1,000 percent," but when the *Washington Post*, the *Los Angeles Times*, and the *New York Times* called for Eagleton to quit, McGovern recanted and asked Eagleton to withdraw from the ticket. McGovern replaced Eagleton with former Peace Corps director and Kennedy in-law Sargent Shriver, and Richard Nixon and Spiro Agnew defeated the two in the biggest landslide in American history.

Littering About

On April 22, 1990, an estimated 750,000 people gathered in Central Park in New York City to celebrate Earth Day. The participants left behind 154.3 tons of litter.

Hip to Time

In the 1969 movie *Easy Rider*, when Peter Fonda hides his money in the gas tank of his motorcycle, he is wearing a pricey Rolex watch. Soon after, to show his disregard for time, he throws away his wristwatch—which has inexplicably changed into a cheap Timex.

"I'm hip to time," says Fonda, who then contradicts himself by insisting that he and costar Dennis Hopper have only two weeks to ride their motorcycles to New Orleans to arrive in time for Mardi Gras.

Lay It on the Line

In 1936, Ecuador erected a granite column to mark the spot where, two hundred years earlier, an expedition commissioned by the French Academy of Sciences identified the equatorial line near the village of San Antonio de Pichincha. The Ecuadorians built the column in the wrong spot—a few hundred yards off the line. In 1986, the government demolished the monument and erected a 100-foot-tall obelisk topped with a brass globe thirteen feet in diameter at the proper latitude.

The Ultimate Lemon

In September 1957, after years of research and millions of dollars in investment costs, the Ford Motor Company spent $10 million on advertising to launch a new line of midsize automobiles—the Edsel, named after the only son of company founder Henry Ford. Unfortunately, at least half of the Edsels purchased were lemons, with problems including malfunctioning doors, faulty brakes and power steering, poor paint jobs, frozen transmissions, and push buttons that stuck in the steering wheel. After three years, Ford had sold only 110,000 Edsels, losing an estimated $350 million.

Par for the Course

President Dwight D. Eisenhower played golf nearly every Sunday on a course near Gettysburg, Pennsylvania. Unbeknownst to Eisenhower, a 1794 state law made it illegal to play golf in Pennsylvania on Sunday. The law was not repealed until 1960.

Out Cold

On January 15, 2000, eighty-year-old George Crowley, inventor of the electric blanket, died of pneumonia.

On the Road to the White House

While running for president of the United States in 2000, Republican candidate George W. Bush pledged to return honor and integrity to the White House. On November 2, 2000, four days before the election, Thomas Connolly, a Maine lawyer and Democratic activist, gave a copy of a 1976 police report to a Portland journalist, revealing that Bush had failed to disclose that he had pleaded guilty to a drunk driving charge in 1976.

All You Need Is Love

Greek philosopher Empedocles (circa 495–435 BCE) claimed that everything in the universe is composed of four elements (earth, air, fire, and water), which he insisted were bonded together by love and driven apart by strife.

Ether Disappears into Thin Air

In the 1600s, scientists claimed that light travels through an invisible, weightless, frictionless, stationary, omnipresent substance called ether, which fills all space. Centuries later, in 1905, Albert Einstein published his theory of relativity, showing that light does not rely on the existence of ether.

What's Good for General Motors

In the 1990s, General Motors steered away from making passenger cars in favor of more profitable trucks and sport utility vehicles. Even after the terrorist attacks on September 11, 2001, the company refused to help reduce America's dependence on foreign oil by manufacturing more fuel-efficient cars. Instead, General Motors continued marketing large, gas-guzzling SUVs and Hummers. When the price of oil skyrocketed and television news stations broadcasted nightly images of decimated Hummers in Iraq, sales plummeted and General Motors teetered on the edge of bankruptcy.

Parallel Thought

Ancient Greek mathematician Euclid assumed that space was flat, and based on this assumption, wrongly concluded that parallel lines never meet. In the nineteenth century, German mathematician Georg Friedrich Bernhard Riemann proved that on the surface of a sphere, parallel lines do meet.

Eugenics for Idiots

In the 1880s, British scientist Sir Francis Galton (1822–1911) called the science of human breeding "eugenics" and urged the planned improvement of the human race by selection of superior parents, erroneously convinced that morals were inherited. In response to eugenics, several European countries and twenty-seven states in America enacted laws to sterilize people with epilepsy, learning disabilities, psychiatric disorders, and criminal records. Under a 1926 law, Sweden sterilized some sixty thousand people identified with undesirable traits. Eugenics also obsessed Adolf Hitler, inciting him to exterminate six million Jews and encourage mating only between pure "Aryans."

Roseanne's Nosedive

In the ninth season of the ABC sitcom *Roseanne*, ranked in the Nielsen top twenty shows for eight years, the working-class Conner family won the state lottery jackpot of $108 million, abandoning the main premise of the show and sending the show plummeting to number thirty-five in the ratings.

Suspended Animation

On Wednesday, September 24, 2008, in response to the nation's financial section collapse, Republican presidential candidate John McCain announced that he was suspending his campaign to return to Washington, D.C., to work on the bailout plan. McCain also insisted that he would not participate in a debate scheduled for that Friday night against Democratic presidential candidate Barack Obama unless Congress passed a bailout plan. After arriving in Washington, McCain admitted that he had not read the three-page proposed bailout. Although he accomplished nothing and a bailout plan had not yet been enacted, McCain relented and showed up at the debate against Obama on Friday night.

A Fallen Angel

Angel Falls, twice the height of the Empire State Building and twenty times as high as Niagara Falls, is named after Jimmie Angel, a U.S. pilot who discovered them cascading from Auyán-Tepuí in Venezuela in 1935. Angel landed his Flamingo G-2-W, *El Rio Caroni*, on top of Auyán-Tepuí in 1937, where it remained for the next forty-three years, embedded in a bog, until the Venezuelan air force rescued the propeller plane.

One and One and One Is Three

A Volkswagen Beetle appears on the cover of the Beatles' 1969 album *Abbey Road*. Its license plate reads "28IF." Some fans, convinced that the Beatles had planted clues on their record albums to suggest that Beatle Paul McCartney was dead, claimed the figures on the plate revealed McCartney's age *if* he were still alive. When *Abbey Road* was released, however, Paul McCartney was twenty-seven years old—not twenty-eight.

Rubber Bands from Heaven

In March 2003, Tony Evans of Swansea, Wales, dropped his one-ton rubber-band ball out of a plane over Arizona to see if it would bounce. The television show *Ripley's Believe It Or Not!* paid for the ball to be dropped above the Mojave Desert, and a skydiving cameraman filmed its descent. The ball took twenty seconds to hit the ground and created a four-foot-wide crater. It did not bounce. Instead, the ball broke apart on impact, leaving the rubber-band remains in the bottom of the crater.

Sea Sick

The Caspian Sea, the Sea of Galilee, the Aral Sea, the Salton Sea, and the Dead Sea are all misnamed. A sea is a body of water connected to the ocean, like the Caribbean Sea, the Mediterranean Sea, and the Arabian Sea. The Caspian Sea, the Sea of Galilee, the Aral

Sea, the Salton Sea, and the Dead Sea are all surrounded by land, making them lakes.

Fool's Paradise

During the 1982 Falklands War, Britain's Royal Air Force claimed that U.S. satellite photographs proved it had effectively bombed Port Stanley's only runway, preventing Argentine forces from flying in supplies. In truth, Argentine soldiers had simply used buckets and shovels to build authentic-looking bomb crater walls to fool satellite cameras. At night, the Argentineans cleared the phony craters to allow supply planes to land and then rebuilt the crater walls before dawn.

Singing the Blues

In 1994, ballyhooed actor David Caruso abandoned his critically acclaimed starring role as Detective John Kelly on the hit television police drama *NYPD Blue* after only four shows in the second season in hopes of achieving movie stardom. His subsequent roles in the box-office flops *Kiss of Death* and *Jade*, combined with his reputation as a prima donna, quashed his movie career. In 2002, he resurfaced on television as Lieutenant Horatio Caine on the television crime drama *CSI: Miami*.

Tipper Stickers

Record companies, in response to pressure from Tipper Gore's Parents' Music Resource Center, now place warning labels on CDs containing explicit lyrics to alert parents that the songs might be inappropriate for minors. Critics argue that the labels, nicknamed Tipper Stickers, have backfired, prompting kids to buy the controversial CDs because of the parent advisory label.

The Sound and the Misspelling

Novelist William Faulkner's last name was actually Falkner. According to some accounts, when the writer's first book, *The Marble Faun*, was published in 1924, the printer mistakenly added the letter *u* to Falkner's name, making it Faulkner. Although miffed, the author simply adopted the new spelling of his name.

Turning into a Pumpkin

In the popular 1950 Walt Disney animated movie *Cinderella*, Cinderella's fairy godmother turns a Rouge Vif d'Etampes pumpkin—developed in France during the late nineteenth century—into a coach. When French writer Charles Perrault told the Cinderella story in his book *The Tales of Mother Goose*, published in 1697, the Rouge Vif d'Etampes pumpkin did not yet exist.

When It Absolutely, Positively Has to Be Obsolete

In 1984, FedEx, having set up a satellite system, introduced Zap Mail as a new document-delivery system service. A FedEx courier would pick up a document, bring it to a nearby FedEx office, and fax it to a FedEx office in the destination city, where another FedEx courier would deliver the faxed copy to the addressee. But around that same time, fax machines suddenly became affordable and businesses began buying their own fax machines, eliminating the need for Zap Mail, which FedEx discontinued in 1986, losing more than $230 million.

The Bank Dick

Afraid of finding himself in a strange town without any money, comedian W. C. Fields opened a bank account in every town he passed through, but remembered only twenty-three out of an estimated seven hundred accounts—misplacing approximately $1.3 million.

What the Fonck

In 1924, when New York City hotel owner Raymond Orteig offered a $25,000 prize to the first person to fly from New York to Paris, French World War I pilot René Fonck had a 38,000-pound, three-engine biplane built at a cost of $105,000. Fonck ignored pleas from the plane's renowned designer, aviation pioneer Igor Sikorsky, to stress-test the plane, which weighed 10,000 pounds over its engineered maximum. On September 21, 1926, when Fonck tried to take off for his journey from New York's Roosevelt Field, the landing gear bent, the rear wheel fell off, and the plane crashed through a fence and burst into flames.

Hanoi Jane

In July 1972, during the Vietnam War, actress and antiwar activist Jane Fonda traveled to Hanoi, where she was photographed smiling and seated behind an antiaircraft gun, made radio appeals for U.S. pilots to stop bombing and return home, and, standing with American prisoners of war at a North Vietnamese–sponsored news conference, told reporters that the North Vietnamese did not torture prisoners. After his release from North Vietnam the following year, former prisoner of war David Hoffman, a navy lieutenant commander who had appeared with Fonda at the Hanoi news conference, revealed that the North Vietnamese had tortured him to force him to participate.

Stamp Out Incompetence

In 1999, the U.S. Postal Service printed 100 million sixty-cent airmail stamps with a caption that incorrectly placed the Grand Canyon in Colorado, rather than Arizona. The Postal Service destroyed the stamps and reprinted them with the correct caption but accidentally flipped the photograph of the Grand Canyon, producing a mirror image of the landmark.

Strange Beliefs

On October 6, 1976, during a televised debate with Democratic presidential nominee Jimmy Carter, President Gerald Ford claimed, "There is no Soviet domination of Eastern Europe, and there never will be under a Ford administration. . . . I don't believe . . . that the Yugoslavians consider themselves dominated by the Soviet Union. I don't believe that the Romanians consider themselves dominated by the Soviet Union. I don't believe that the Poles consider themselves dominated by the Soviet Union. Each of these countries is independent, autonomous, it has its own territorial integrity, and the United States does not concede that those countries are under the domination of the Soviet Union." At the time, the Soviet Union controlled Yugoslavia, Romania, and Poland.

The Story of a Man Named Brady

In 1974, when the television sitcom *The Brady Bunch* began sagging in the ratings in its fifth season, producer Sherwood Schwartz, pressured by the network to win back a younger audience by infusing the show with young blood, added nine-year-old Cousin Oliver (played by Robbie Rist). After six episodes with cloying Cousin Oliver, ABC-TV canceled the series.

Power Trip

After Libyans rose up in protest against his dictatorship on February 20, 2011, strongman Muammar Gadhafi claimed that all the Libyan people loved him, and insisted he could not step down because he did not have an official position and that power rested with the people.

The tyrant also declared that the protesters were youths acting under the influence of hallucinogenic drugs supplied by Osama bin Laden through Al Qaeda. "Their ages are seventeen," said Gadhafi on February 25. "They give them pills at night, they put hallucinatory pills in their drinks, their milk, their coffee, their Nescafé." On March 3, the Libyan government revealed a massive shipment of 36 million confiscated pills, which turned out to be tramadol, a painkiller whose worst side effects are drowsiness and constipation.

Pinto Problems

The Ford Motor Company introduced its compact Pinto automobile in Brazil, unaware that the car's name was a slang term in Portuguese for "small penis." Ford changed the name of the car to Corcel, Portuguese for "horse."

Viva Quicksand!

When Mexican revolutionary general Rodolfo Fierro, marching toward Sonora with Pancho Villa's troops in 1917, decided to take a shortcut, his horse got caught in quicksand. Fierro, loaded down with gold, sank to his death.

The Old College Try

Addressing the audience at a fund-raiser at California State University, Stanislaus, on June 25, 2010, former Alaska governor Sarah Palin said, "This is Reagan country and . . . perhaps it was destiny that the man who went to California's Eureka College would become so woven within and interlinked to the Golden State." Reagan did attend Eureka College—in Eureka, Illinois.

Henry Ford's Six Cents

In 1916, an editorial in the *Chicago Daily Tribune*, misinformed about the Ford Motor Company's policy on paying its employees for their National Guard service, called Henry Ford "an ignorant idealist" and "an anarchistic enemy of the nation." Ford promptly sued for libel for $1 million. Instead of focusing on the term *anarchist*, which had already been ruled libelous, Ford's lawyer, Alfred Lucking, tried to prove that Ford was not ignorant. During the 1919 trial, defense attorney Elliott Stevenson got Ford to claim that the American Revolution occurred in 1812, that chili con carne is "a large mobile army," and that Benedict Arnold was "a writer." The jury awarded Ford six cents.

Famous Last Words

During the O. J. Simpson murder trial, Los Angeles Police Department detective Mark Fuhrman swore under oath on March 15, 1995, that he had not used a specific racial epithet during the past ten years. Screenwriter and professor Laura Hart McKinny provided defense attorneys with thirteen hours of taped interviews with Fuhrman conducted between 1985 and 1994 in which Fuhrman used the racial epithet forty-two times, proving that Fuhrman had lied under oath and discrediting him as a reliable witness against O. J. Simpson.

Better Late Than Never

In 1633, the Vatican summoned astronomer Galileo Galilei (1564–1642) before the Inquisition and threatened to burn him at the stake for stating that the earth revolves around the sun in his 1632 book, *Dialogue Concerning the Two Chief World Systems.* To save his life, Galileo renounced his discovery and spent the remaining eight years of his life under house arrest. A mere 359 years later, on October 30, 1992, Pope John Paul II, having conducted a thirteen-year investigation into the matter, formally stated that the Church was wrong to have condemned Galileo.

Ding-a-lings

When assassin Charles Guiteau shot President James A. Garfield on July 2, 1881, a doctor at the scene poured brandy and ammonia down Garfield's throat, causing the wounded president to vomit. Garfield was taken to the White House, where Dr. Willard Bliss inserted a Nelaton probe into the wound to find the bullet slug, but succeeded only in damaging more tissue when the probe got stuck in the shattered fragments of Garfield's eleventh rib. Bliss inserted his unwashed finger in the wound, as did other doctors, infecting it. Inventor Alexander Graham Bell showed up with a telephone receiver wired to a metal detector to help locate the slug, but when doctors cut open the deep spot indicated by Bell, the slug was not there. Garfield died on September 19, 1881. The autopsy revealed that the slug had been enveloped by a protective cyst, four inches from Garfield's spine, and would have been relatively harmless.

Genuine Baby Food

Gerber started selling baby food in Africa, using the same packaging as in the United States—with an illustration of the Gerber baby on the label. Unfortunately, in Africa, companies label jars and bottles of food with pictures of the ingredients they contain.

Sit Right Back and You'll Hear a Tale

In 1964, the entire cast of the television sitcom *Gilligan's Island*, convinced that the series about seven castaways stranded on a Pacific island would bomb, opted for straight salaries rather than a percentage of the show's profits. Although the hit series was rerun in syndication for decades, the cast members remained stranded without any royalties or further payment.

Please Don't Squeeze the President

In 1978, a survey conducted by Procter & Gamble revealed that Mr. Whipple, the fictional spokesperson for Charmin toilet tissue, was the third most recognized face in America after former president Richard Nixon and evangelist Billy Graham. According to the survey, more Americans recognized Mr. Whipple than prevailing United States president Jimmy Carter.

Galloping Gertie

On November 7, 1940, four months after the ribbon was cut on the $6.5 million Tacoma Narrows Bridge in Washington, a 42-mile-per-hour wind created oscillations in the suspension bridge (then the third longest in the world), tearing several suspenders loose and causing the single 2,800-foot span to break apart and fall into Puget

Sound. Engineers had designed "Galloping Gertie" without taking into account aerodynamic effects and other structural weaknesses.

The Shock of His Life

In 1989, 28-year-old convicted murderer Michael Anderson Godwin, having avoided the electric chair through legal appeals, bit into an electrical cord to fix a pair of headphones while sitting naked on a steel toilet in his South Carolina prison cell and accidentally electrocuted himself.

Gone with the Stork

In the 1939 movie *Gone with the Wind*, Melanie's pregnancy, when calculated by the dates of the Civil War battles mentioned, lasts twenty-one months.

Smoke Signals

In 1742, American statesman and scientist Benjamin Franklin invented the Pennsylvania Fireplace, a stove he thought would be more efficient by drawing smoke from the bottom rather than the top. The smoke, however, refused to defy the laws of heat convection (namely that hot air rises), making the stove inoperable.

Saving Money at All Costs

In September 1993, Vice President Al Gore, assigned to find ways to make the government run more efficiently, released copies of a 168-page report titled *Creating a Government That Works Better and Costs Less*, printed by the Government Printing Office for $168,915 (approximately $4 a copy). According to an internal memo from the Government Printing Office, the printing bill would have been only $54,091 (roughly $0.90 per copy) had the report not been "produced on the best and most expensive Grade 1 coated paper (high gloss) in multiple ink colors, at Quality Level 2 (on a scale of 1 to 5) on a rush schedule over the Labor Day weekend."

All Washed Up

Since full-body bathing required nudity, the Church in the Middle Ages labeled the activity as sinful, banning the temptation of the flesh and putting an end to regular bathing throughout Europe. Without good hygiene, diseases like the Black Death spread like wildfire, killing millions.

Down in the Mouth

On June 27, 1995, actor Hugh Grant, having been propelled to Hollywood stardom by the 1994 movie *Four Weddings and a Funeral*, was arrested after being discovered in a compromising position in his car on Sunset Boulevard in Hollywood with a prostitute named Divine Brown. When Grant appeared on *The Tonight Show* two weeks later, host Jay Leno began the interview by asking, "What were you thinking?" The incident tarnished Grant's Hollywood career for several years and irreparably damaged his relationship with longtime live-in girlfriend Elizabeth Hurley.

Winging It

In 1869, French naturalist Etienne Leopold Trouvelot, living in Medford, Massachusetts, imported gypsy moth caterpillars from France in hopes of crossbreeding the gypsy moth with the American silk moth to create a silkworm capable of making a durable thread. Descendants of those gypsy moth caterpillars frequently defoliate millions of acres of trees in New England.

A Federal Case

On November 2, 2000, four days before the presidential election, Republican nominee George W. Bush stated that Democrats "want the federal government controlling Social Security, like it's some kind of federal program." Social Security is a federal program.

Flying Toast

Around 1500 CE, Chinese inventor Wan Hu attempted to fly by building a plane made from two kites, a chair, and forty-two rocket-like fireworks. When the firecrackers were ignited, Wan Hu and his contraption went up in flames.

Jumping the Gun

In March 1981, when a would-be assassin wounded President Ronald Reagan in the chest, Secretary of State Alexander Haig, a retired four-star general, held a press conference in the White House briefing room. When asked, "Who's making the decisions?" he replied: "Constitutionally, gentlemen, you have the president, the vice president, and secretary of state in that order and should the president decide he wants to transfer the helm to the vice president, he will do so. He has not done that. As of now, I am in control here, in the White House, pending the return of the vice president." Haig failed to recall that next in line to the presidency is the vice president, followed by the speaker of the house, the president pro tempore of the Senate, and *then* the secretary of state.

Tell Me What You Really Really Want

In May 1998, Geri Halliwell, a member of the Spice Girls—the English pop girl group with the highest grossing concert tour of 1998, the best-selling album by a female group in music history, and the box-office hit movie *Spice World*—left the group to pursue a solo career. Halliwell's departure killed the Spice Girls' momentum, and her solo career quickly fizzled.

His Big Break

At the 1980 Kuhmo Chamber Music Festival, Soviet cellist Augustinas Vasiliauskas rose to the podium for a third time to bow to the audience for their standing ovation. He tripped, fell, and smashed his 300-year-old Ruggieri cello.

Monkey Business

In an interview published in the *New York Times* on May 3, 1987, Senator Gary Hart of Colorado, a married man and the front-runner for the 1988 Democratic presidential nomination, responded to rumors that he was having an extramarital affair with a dare: "Follow me around. I don't care. I'm serious. If anybody wants to put a tail on me, go ahead. They'll be very bored." That same day, the *Miami Herald* reported that Hart had spent the night of May 2 at his Washington townhouse with 29-year-old salesperson and part-time actress and model Donna Rice, compelling Hart to drop out of the presidential race a week later. On May 25, the *National Enquirer* published an incriminating photograph of Donna Rice sitting on Gary Hart's lap in Bimini aboard a chartered yacht, aptly named *Monkey Business*.

Say What?

In 1988, Senator Orrin Hatch of Utah said, "Capital punishment is our society's recognition of the sanctity of human life."

For Heaven's Sake

In 1979, United Artists executives allowed Academy Award–winning writer-director Michael Cimino to hire his girlfriend, Joann Carelli, as line producer on his budgeted $11.6-million western, *Heaven's Gate*, to make sure the production stayed on budget. Carelli allowed cost overruns on *Heaven's Gate*—a movie without any major stars or special effects—to escalate to a record $45 million.

Cimino kept his crew on call twelve to eighteen hours a day, seven days a week, paying five times the average union wage. He had the western town built at his Montana location completely torn down and rebuilt because he wanted to widen the street by six feet. Cimino shot 1.5 million feet of film (fifteen times the average) and printed 500 hours worth of film to be edited down to 3 hours, 39 minutes.

When critics panned the New York premiere on November 18, 1980, United Artists pulled the film from theaters, re-edited it down to 2 hours, 28 minutes, and rereleased it five months later, on April 23, 1981. Despite heavy promotion, the movie bombed, putting United Artists on the brink of bankruptcy, until MGM bought the studio.

Losing Her Grip

In 1922, Ernest Hemingway's first wife, Hadley, decided to join her husband for Christmas in Switzerland, where he was working as a news correspondent. As a surprise, she brought a suitcase packed with all of the copies of Hemingway's untitled first novel and several unpublished short stories. At the Paris railroad station, the suitcase was stolen.

Dead End

On October 5, 1971, British intelligence chief Sir Peregrine Henniker-Heaton told his wife he was going for a morning walk and then disappeared. Scotland Yard spent three years searching for him, convinced he had been abducted and possibly killed by foreign agents. In June 1974, Henniker-Heaton's twenty-year-old son, Yvo, found his father's skeleton and a suicide note in a locked study in his seventeen-room West London home.

Pee-wee's Big Adventure

On July 26, 1991, comedian Paul Reubens—who starred as the nerdy Pee-wee Herman on the hit Saturday morning children's show *Pee-wee's Playhouse* and in the movie *Pee-wee's Big Adventure*—was arrested for indecent exposure after a plainclothes detective allegedly caught him masturbating at a screening of the X-rated films *Catalina Five-O: Tiger Shark* and *Nurse Nancy* at the South Trail

Adult Theater in Sarasota, Florida. CBS promptly dropped remaining episodes of *Pee-wee's Playhouse*, and all Pee-wee-related merchandise was pulled from shelves—sending his skyrocketing career into an abrupt nosedive.

Dream On

In ancient Greece, ill people slept in the temples of Asclepius, convinced that the god of medicine would appear in their dreams and cure them. The only thing it cured was cabin fever.

Putting the Cart Before the Horse

In 1898, Dr. Heinrich Dreser, head of the drug research laboratory at the Bayer company in Germany, announced that he had developed diacetylmorphine—a nonaddictive derivative of morphine with four to eight times the painkilling power. Bayer marketed diacetylmorphine under the brand name Heroin (derived from the "heroic" state of mind the drug purportedly induced), and the new drug was used in cough syrups and pain remedies, and prescribed by doctors for headaches and menstrual cramps. In 1910, doctors realized that heroin, which had been on the market for twelve years, is far more addictive than morphine. In 1924, the United States banned the manufacture of heroin, but by then there were plenty of addicts to create a demand for the drug on the black market.

Hippocratic Nonsense

Greek physician Hippocrates (circa 460–377 BCE), considered the father of modern medicine, incorrectly claimed:

- North winds cause constipation.

- People with speech impediments are more likely to get protracted diarrhea.

- People suffering from jaundice are not susceptible to flatulence.

- The sex of an unborn child can be determined based on which one of the mother's breasts becomes larger.

- Bald people who get varicose veins regain their hair.

- Veins carry hot air (not blood).

- Disease is caused by vapors secreted by undigested foods from unsuitable diets.

For the Love of Leibniz

German philosopher Gottfried Wilhelm Leibniz (1646–1716) insisted in his book *Théodicée*, published in 1710, that everything is for the best in this, the best of all possible worlds, because God created the universe. Leibniz's philosophy came crashing down in 1755, when an earthquake in Lisbon, Portugal, killed some sixty thousand people, including many who died in the rubble of the churches where they had been observing All Saints' Day. French writer Voltaire lambasted Leibniz's philosophy in his book *Candide*, caricaturing Leibniz's adherents through the character Dr. Pangloss, an absurdly overzealous optimist.

Wake Up and Smell the Coffee

On the night of June 5, 1944, German dictator Adolf Hitler took sleeping pills and gave orders that he not be woken. At dawn on June 6, the Allied Forces launched their D-Day invasion of Normandy Beach with parachute landings. German general Gerd von Rundstedt immediately ordered two panzer divisions to defend the region. However, German headquarters in Berlin ordered that von Rundstedt halt the two panzer divisions—until he received direct authorization from Adolf Hitler. When Hitler finally woke up, the Allies had won the invasion.

Tub of Lard

William Howard Taft, who weighed 332 pounds, was the only United States president to get stuck in the White House bathtub. After being pried out by two men, Taft installed an oversized bathtub that measured seven feet long and forty-one inches wide and could accommodate four people at the same time.

Wrapped in the Flag

On March 28, 1970, Yippie cofounder Abbie Hoffman appeared on *The Merv Griffin Show* wearing an American-flag shirt. CBS network officials electronically blotted out Hoffman and the shirt with a blue square. More than two thousand viewers called CBS to object to the censoring, protests took place in front of CBS offices in three cities, and Merv Griffin publicly apologized. Prior to Hoffman's appearance, Ricky Nelson, Raquel Welch, Roy Rogers, and Ryan O'Neal had worn similar shirts on television.

Look, Mom, No Teeth!

For some four hundred years, beginning in the fourteenth century, barber-surgeons in Europe whitened teeth with a solution of nitric acid, which destroyed the enamel, causing cavities.

Lost Cause

For centuries, doctors insisted that ulcers resulted from stress and bad eating habits. Research has shown that a bacterium called *Helicobacter pylori* actually causes more than 90 percent of duodenal ulcers and up to 80 percent of gastric ulcers. The bacterium seems to weaken the mucous tissue in the stomach, making it vulnerable to digestive acids.

Weathering the Storm

On September 2, 2005, in the aftermath of the devastation caused by Hurricane Katrina and the widely reported failures and incompetence of the Federal Emergency Management Agency (FEMA) to provide adequate relief to the victims in New Orleans and along the Gulf Coast, President George W. Bush lauded FEMA director Michael D. Brown on national television. "Brownie," he said, "you're doing a heck of a job." Ten days later, after continued media coverage revealed that Brown, who had been forced to resign from his previous position as judges and stewards commissioner of the International Arabian Horse Association, was indeed doing a heck of a job bungling the disaster response, Brown resigned in disgrace—although Bush kept his inept crony on salary, at $148,000 a year.

Urine Trouble

Ancient Romans used urine as mouthwash and as an ingredient in toothpaste—convinced that urine whitened teeth. This practice continued until the eighteenth century. The active ingredient in urine that whitens teeth is ammonia, which could have been added to toothpastes and mouthwashes independently, without the need for urine.

Forever Young

Spanish explorer Ponce de León searched Florida for the mythical Fountain of Youth, a spring whose waters would reputedly make old people young and heal the sick. He did find a spring in St. Augustine that he thought would give him eternal youth, and today you can visit the Fountain of Youth at 11 Magnolia Avenue and admire a statue of Ponce de León whose features do not age.

Switch to Creamy

In 1972, the Oregon Health Department discovered that many of the chunks in Hoody's Chunky Style Peanut Butter were actually rat droppings.

Hoover Vacuums Suck

In 1993, the Hoover vacuum cleaner company offered consumers in Great Britain and Ireland two free round-trip airline tickets worth up to $600 with the purchase of a new Hoover vacuum cleaner or washing machine priced over $150—or two round-trip tickets to New York or Orlando with the purchase of $375 worth of Hoover appliances. When more than 200,000 customers tried to claim their free tickets, Hoover's travel agents added unreasonable restrictions (such as inconvenient airports and undesirable departure dates) to the deal, provoking public outrage. Hoover's parent company, Maytag, fired three top Hoover executives and set up a fund to pay for more than 400,000 round-trip tickets, costing the company some $50 million.

Happy Hour

The Uape Indians, of the upper Amazon in Brazil, mix the ashes of their cremated dead with *casiri*, a beer made from manioc. The mourners drink the beverage in hopes of absorbing all the good qualities of the dearly departed. Bottoms up!

Defaming Debendox

In June 1982, William McBride, the Australian obstetrician who two decades earlier revealed that the prescription sedative thalidomide caused severe birth deformities, published a paper in the *Australian Journal of Biological Sciences* claiming that hyoscine, an ingredient in the morning-sickness drug Debendox (sold as Bendectin in the United States), caused birth defects in rabbits. Faced with hundreds of lawsuits, drug manufacturer Merrell Dow withdrew Debendox from the market. In 1986, an investigation revealed that McBride had altered the data provided by his assistants, which showed that Debendox had no adverse effects. In 1993, a medical tribunal found McBride guilty of scientific fraud.

Bed-wetting Cure

As early as 77 BCE, the Roman scholar Pliny the Elder suggested adding boiled mice to the food of children who wet the bed to cure incontinence.

The Disease Ain't the Cure

In his 1811 book *Organon of the Rational Art of Healing*, German doctor Samuel Hahnemann (1755–1843) wrongly insisted: "A disease can only be destroyed and cured by a remedy which has a tendency to produce a similar disease, for the effects of drugs are in themselves no other than artificial diseases." Hahnemann named this process homeopathy, and this alleged science, while proven ineffective, is practiced to this very day.

It's Raining Hot Dogs

On April 18, 2000, during a Toronto Blue Jays baseball game at the SkyDome, a Hot Dog Blaster, a device used by vendors to shoot hot dogs to sports fans, malfunctioned, showering the fans with pieces of hot dogs and buns.

Speak Now or Forever Hold Your Peace

On December 15, 1924, in a letter to British prime minister Stanley Baldwin, future British prime minister Winston Churchill wrote: "I do not believe there is the slightest chance of war with Japan in our lifetime. The Japanese are our allies. . . . Japan is at the other end of the world. She cannot menace our vital security in any way. . . . War with Japan is not a possibility which any reasonable government need take into account." Seventeen years later, on December 8, 1941, Britain declared war on Japan.

Christmas Bash

On December 24, 1994, the Christmas twins, 31-year-old sisters Lorraine and Levinia Christmas, crashed head-on as they headed to each other's homes in Flitcham, England, to deliver Christmas presents. The Christmas twins suffered chest injuries, whiplash, and concussions. "We did a double take when we first received details of the accident," a police spokesman told the Reuters news service. "We thought it was a practical joke."

Where the Sun Doesn't Shine

April 19, 1965, marked the opening of the Houston Astrodome, built for $30 million. The 4,596 transparent plastic panels in the dome itself allowed sunlight in, but not without creating massive glare. Ultimately, the only way to eliminate the glare was to paint the panels a dark color, keeping out the sunlight entirely.

Hubble Trouble

On April 24, 1990, NASA launched a space shuttle mission to place the $1.6-billion Hubble telescope into space—only to discover that the telescope's primary 2.4-meter diameter parabolic mirror had been ground to the wrong shape. Technicians had accidentally dropped some twenty-five-cent washers into the telescope's optical testing device, unwittingly throwing a small compensating lens (used during testing) out of whack by 1.3 millimeters. To save money, NASA had decided against running optical tests on the lens before the launch. Had the error been detected on earth, the shape of the lens could have been corrected for approximately $2 million. Instead, NASA launched a special space shuttle mission to fit the Hubble telescope with a corrective lens—at a cost to taxpayers of nearly $86 million.

A Mind of His Own

In 1968, Vice President Hubert H. Humphrey told *Playboy* magazine, "No sane person in the country likes the war in Vietnam, and neither does President Johnson."

A Match Made in Hell

In 1830, French chemist Charles Sauria developed phosphorus matches, inadvertently giving rise to "phossy jaw," a fatal disease technically known as phosphorus necrosis and primarily affecting factory workers. Highly poisonous, phosphorus essentially causes bones to disintegrate and deform. The phosphorus scraped from the heads of a pack of matches could also be used to commit suicide or murder.

Major Boobs

Hunt-Wesson introduced its line of Big John TV dinners in French Canada as Gros Jos, unaware that in Quebec the slang phrase means "big breasts."

IBM Sings the Blues

In 1980, as IBM raced to build a personal computer, Microsoft founders Bill Gates and Paul Allen offered to sell the rights to their MS-DOS operating system to IBM, but IBM declined, deciding instead to lease the operating system. Microsoft then went on to license MS-DOS to computer companies building IBM clones, making the operating system the industry standard and turning Microsoft into a corporate giant.

A Doll Without a Doll House

In 2009, American Girl, LLC introduced a "less fortunate" American Girl doll named Gwen Thompson, whose mother details the doll's destitute lifestyle in an accompanying storybook: "At first, my daughter and I slept in our car. I'd park so that we'd wake up near a wayside rest area or restaurant—somewhere where we could use the sink for washing up—and then I'd go to work and pretend that life was just as it had always been." When winter arrived, Gwen's mother brought them to Sunrise House, a place for homeless women and children, enabling them to get back on their feet and move into a new apartment. The limited-edition doll sold for $95, and children could pay to have Gwen's hair done at the American Girl store for a mere $20.

When the Chips Are Down

In 1994, the Intel Corporation, discovering that a flaw in its Pentium chip affected computer calculations, insisted that no problem existed. When a huge number of consumers provided the company with evidence of the flaw, Intel claimed the problem would affect only one out of every nine billion calculations. In truth, the flaw caused a mistake every few minutes, prompting IBM to stop shipping computers installed with the Pentium chip. Finally, Intel recalled the Pentium chip, agreeing to replace some six million chips—for a loss of $500 million.

Up the River Without a Paddle

In 1983, the Intermarine Company, of Amèglia, Italy, contracted by the Malaysian government to build four large ships, completed and launched a minesweeper and three military launchers from its shipyard on the Magra River, a mile from the Mediterranean Sea. However, all four of the ships were too tall to pass under the Colombiera Bridge, which crosses the Magra River. The Intermarine Company then proposed to dismantle the bridge, sail the ships to the Mediterranean, and rebuild the bridge—but the local council refused to grant permission.

Let It Snow

In the 1933 film *The Invisible Man*, Claude Rains becomes invisible, except for his clothes. At the end of the film, he strips naked to escape from the police, but the cops follow his footprints in the snow—footprints made by shoes that the invisible man was not wearing.

The Bare Bones

In 1912, amateur paleontologist Charles Dawson, having found fragments of a skull and jawbone at Barkham Manor on Piltdown Common near Lewes, England, claimed that the remnants belonged to a single human, whom he called *Eoanthropus dawsoni* ("Dawson's dawn man")—a strange combination of man and ape from the Pliocene period, two to five million years ago. The skull and jawbone, hailed as the missing link in Darwin's theory of evolution, became known as the Piltdown Man.

In 1949, British Museum geologist Dr. Kenneth Oakley analyzed the fluorine content of the fossil bones and determined that the Piltdown skull and jaw were no more than six hundred years old, while the animal teeth associated with them were genuine fossils that came from a variety of locations and time periods. In 1953, Oxford University anthropologist J. S. Weiner identified the cranium as human, recognized the jaw and teeth as belonging to an orangutan, and determined that the teeth had been filed down to imitate human wear. Weiner suspected that Dawson had perpetrated the hoax for the glory of making a major scientific discovery.

A Bang-up Celebration

On August 20, 1988, Iraqis celebrated the end of the eight-year war against Iran by firing guns into the air for the next three days. Bullets falling back to earth killed 350 Iraqis.

A Big Smash Hit

On September 8, 2004, NASA's *Genesis* spacecraft jettisoned a capsule back to earth with samples of solar wind ions, but the capsule's parachute failed to open, sending the craft and its precious cargo slamming into the Utah desert at nearly one hundred miles per hour. Investigators determined that the capsule's deceleration sensors had been designed upside down.

The Unauthorized Author

In 1971, McGraw-Hill and Time Life paid $1 million to author Clifford Irving for his authorized autobiography of reclusive billionaire Howard Hughes. When Hughes denied any involvement or contact with Irving and obtained an injunction against the book's publication, Irving was convicted of fraud, was forced to pay back the advance to his publisher, and served fourteen months in federal prison.

Seeing the Light

In 1666, English scientist Sir Isaac Newton theorized that light consists of tiny particles called corpuscles that travel in straight lines though space. In 1801, English physicist Thomas Young proved Newton wrong, demonstrating conclusively that particles of light travel in waves.

Mission Exaggerated

On May 1, 2003, President George W. Bush, wearing full flight gear, landed on the deck of the aircraft carrier USS *Abraham Lincoln*, received an enthusiastic reception, and delivered a triumphant speech in front of a banner reading "Mission Accomplished," signaling the end to "major combat operations" in the Iraq invasion. As the insurgent war dragged on, the White House insisted that the crew, not Bush aides, had hung the banner—despite the fact that when the president landed on the aircraft carrier, White House aides had boasted that they had positioned the lectern so that news cameras would see the banner in the background when Bush gave his speech.

Made in Japan

In June 1964, Congressman Charles Joelson of New Jersey announced on the floor of the House of Representatives that souvenir statuettes sold at the Iwo Jima memorial at Arlington National

Cemetery, commemorating the 5,563 marines who had died and the 17,343 marines wounded capturing the island from the Japanese during World War II, had been made in Japan.

Take Manhattan

In 1626, the Canarsie Indians traded the island now known as Manhattan to Dutch colonizer Peter Minuit in exchange for cloth, beads, hatchets, and other assorted trinkets worth sixty Dutch guilders (valued at $24 in the nineteenth century). In 2008, Matthew Mondanile, senior managing director of valuation services at global commercial real estate firm Cushman & Wakefield, told *Forbes* magazine that he estimated Manhattan to be worth $1 trillion.

All Fired Up

On August 8, 1993, to celebrate the Bolivian soccer team's victory over Uruguay in a World Cup qualifying match, fans in the Bolivian village of Ixiamas threw firecrackers into the air—setting fire to the thatched roofs of their huts and burning most of the small village to the ground.

Left Holding the Baby

In 1998, civil rights activist and former Democratic presidential candidate Jesse Jackson, a Baptist minister, served as spiritual adviser to President Bill Clinton to help the nation's leader make amends to his family and country for his extramarital affair with White House intern Monica Lewinsky. On January 18, 2001, the *New York Post* revealed that Jackson, married twenty-nine years with five children, had sired a child out of wedlock with a former staffer twenty years his junior. Jackson admitted to fathering the twenty-month-old baby, revealing that he had been having an extramarital affair while counseling Clinton during the Lewinsky scandal.

Anatomy of a Censor

In 1959, Chicago mayor Richard Daley banned the newly released movie *Anatomy of a Murder*, which deals with a rape trial and contains the spoken words *intercourse* and *contraceptive*. The film, directed by Otto Preminger and starring Jimmy Stewart, was nominated for seven Academy Awards, including Best Picture.

Bringing Up the Rear

During the 1990 primary campaign for Florida governor, Democratic candidate Bill Nelson, in an attempt to force his opponent, Lawton Chiles, to reveal all his health records, disclosed that he had once suffered from hemorrhoids. Chiles won the election.

Start Me Up

In an interview in the 1970s, Rolling Stone Mick Jagger said, "I'd rather be dead than singing 'Satisfaction' when I'm forty-five." Since turning forty-five years old in 1988, Jagger has sung "Satisfaction" on several Rolling Stones world tours.

Promoting Elvis

In the 1957 movie *Jailhouse Rock*, Elvis Presley wears a prison uniform numbered 6239. Later in the film he wears number 6240.

The Power of Witchcraft

On September 18, 2010, comedian Bill Maher aired on his television show *Real Time with Bill Maher* a previously unaired clip from 1999 in which Delaware Republican Senate candidate Christine O'Donnell said, "I dabbled into witchcraft. I hung around people who were doing these things. I'm not making this stuff up." On October 4, O'Donnell launched her first television commercial in her race against Democrat Chris Coons. The ad begins with O'Donnell declaring directly to camera, "I'm not a witch. I'm nothing you've heard. I'm you." Coons won the election with 57 percent of the vote.

The Wit and Wisdom of Dan Quayle

And Levity Is the Soul of Wit

"Verbosity leads to unclear, inarticulate things."

—INTERVIEW WITH
THE ASSOCIATED PRESS,
NOVEMBER 30, 1988

Never Mind

"What a waste it is to lose one's mind—or not to have a mind. How true that is."

—SPEECH TO THE UNITED NEGRO
COLLEGE FUND, WHOSE MOTTO IS
"A MIND IS A TERRIBLE THING TO
WASTE," MAY 9, 1989

The Times They Are A-Changin'

"I believe we are on an irreversible trend toward more freedom and democracy—but that could change."

—ADDRESSING A LONDON NEWSPAPER
SOCIETY FORUM ON EUROPE, MAY 22, 1989

You Can Say That Again

"I stand by all the misstatements that I've made."

—TO *ABC NEWS* WHITE HOUSE
CORRESPONDENT SAM DONALDSON,
AUGUST 17, 1989

Is That a Fact?

"Quite frankly, teachers are the only profession that teach our children."

—SPEECH ON PUBLIC EDUCATION TO THE
HUDSON INSTITUTE, SEPTEMBER 18, 1990

Prepared for Nothing

"We are ready for any unforeseen event that may or may not occur."

—TO CLEVELAND'S *PLAIN DEALER*,
SEPTEMBER 22, 1990

Family Values

On May 19, 1992, in a San Francisco speech, Vice President Dan Quayle blamed the violence of the Los Angeles riots on the decay of family values, citing Murphy Brown's decision to give birth out of wedlock and raise the child without a father. Murphy Brown was a fictional character on the television sitcom of the same name.

A Golden Blunder

In 1607, the settlers at Jamestown, Virginia, the first colony in the New World, mined gold and sent a shipload back to London, where assayers identified the glittering metal as iron pyrite, better known as "fool's gold."

The Body Politic

On November 5, 1991, Peter Jennings reported on ABC's *World News Tonight* that Russia would attempt to raise funds by auctioning off the embalmed body of Soviet leader V. I. Lenin, which had been on display in a glass case in a tomb on Red Square since the Soviet leader's death in 1924. The next day in Moscow, Soviet interior minister Viktor Barannikov denounced the story as "an impudent lie." Jennings later retracted the story. He had believed an article written by Christopher Buckley that appeared in *Forbes* magazine's quarterly supplement, *FYI*, as a spoof.

A Trip Down Memory Lane

To protest the 1968 Democratic National Convention in Chicago, Yippie leaders Abbie Hoffman and Jerry Rubin announced that they were considering putting LSD in the city's water supply. In response, Mayor Richard Daley sent thousands of National Guard troops to surround the city's reservoirs and pumping stations—despite being informed by the FBI that lacing the city's water supply with LSD was technologically impossible.

The Straight Dope

On September 28, 1980, the *Washington Post* ran a story titled "Jimmy's World," by Janet Cooke, about an eight-year-old African-American heroin addict whose mother was a former prostitute. The resulting public outcry pressured the police to find little Jimmy, but after a three-week search, the police concluded that the boy did not exist. Cooke refused to identify her sources, claiming drug dealers had threatened her life, and the *Washington Post* stood behind her story. Six months later, Cooke won the Pulitzer Prize for the article. The resulting media attention uncovered the fact that Cooke had lied about her academic credentials on her résumé, prompting her to confess that she had fabricated the entire story, offer a public apology, and resign from the newspaper.

Out the Window

In 1973, winds and bad engineering caused hundreds of window-panes to fall out of Boston's newly built, sixty-story John Hancock Tower, designed by renowned architect I. M. Pei, and crash to the street below. I. M. Pei & Partners replaced all 10,340 windows—at a cost of more than $5 million.

Ahead of His Time

English writer Samuel Johnson (1709–1784) incorrectly claimed, "The cause of baldness in men is dryness of the brain, and its shrinking from the skull."

Take Your Pick

In 1984, the Houston Rockets got the number one pick in the NBA draft of college basketball players, choosing seven-foot-tall Hakeem Olajuwon—rather than University of North Carolina jump shooter Michael Jordan. The Portland Trail Blazers made the second pick, selecting seven-foot-tall Sam Bowie. Finally, the Chicago Bulls chose Jordan, making the future basketball superstar the number three NBA pick.

Rudolph the Radioactive Reindeer

On Christmas Day in 1962, the USSR detonated a nuclear bomb in a test at Novaya Zemlya, a pair of islands inhabited by reindeer in the Arctic Ocean—an unusual way to promote religious tolerance and peace on earth.

Hop to It

In 1770, English explorer Captain James Cook (1728–1779) landed in Australia and asked the aborigines what they called the large marsupials indigenous to the continent. He was told "kangaroo," which, unbeknownst to Cook, is aborigine for "I don't know."

When Irish Eyes Are Lying

In December 2001, after hiring George O'Leary as head football coach of the Notre Dame Fighting Irish for a reported $1.8 million per year, the University discovered outright lies on his résumé. O'Leary claimed that he had lettered three times playing football at the University of New Hampshire, but the school reported he had never played in a game. He also declared that he had received a master's degree from NYU–Stony Brook University, a school that does not exist. After one week in his new job, O'Leary was forced to resign.

Snuffing Out the Painkiller

In 2008, upon learning that one of its adult Motrin products was defective, Johnson & Johnson's McNeil Consumer Healthcare unit hired a private contractor to go into stores across some forty states and secretly buy more than 88,000 Motrin tablets off the shelves without announcing a recall—to avoid alerting the public and news media. The "phantom recall" came to light during congressional hearings regarding Johnson & Johnson's recall of more than 135 million bottles of children's over-the-counter pain medicine, some of which contained tiny particles of metal. The Food and Drug Administration and the U.S. Department of Justice placed McNeil Consumer Heathcare under a consent decree for five years, requiring the company to adhere to a strict timetable in bringing its manufacturing operations back up to standard.

Shotgun Wedding

On October 23, 1986, seven bridegrooms at a wedding in Peshawar, Pakistan, fired their rifles into the air, accidentally shooting down a Pakistan International Airlines plane, killing thirteen passengers and injuring twenty. Pakistani authorities arrested the seven bridegrooms and charged them with "lethal celebrations during marriage ceremonies."

Restoring Arrogance

On August 28, 2010, conservative political commentator Glenn Beck held his "Restoring Honor" rally on the steps of the Lincoln Memorial in Washington, D.C., on the same spot as and on the forty-seventh anniversary of Dr. Martin Luther King's historic "I Have a Dream" speech, sparking fierce criticism. Beck insisted that the event, featuring former Republican vice presidential candidate Sarah Palin and attended by Tea Party members, was apolitical and not racially divisive. Beck told his talk show listeners that "at least 500,000" people had attended his rally. However, AirPhotosLive .com, a firm hired by CBS News, estimated the crowd at between 78,000 and 96,000. To spoof Beck's event, comedian Jon Stewart held a "Rally to Restore Sanity" on October 20, 2010, on the National Mall in Washington, D.C., which, according to AirPhotosLive .com, attracted an estimated 215,000 attendees—more than twice the number of people who attended Beck's rally.

Chicken Fingers

In 1987, when Kentucky Fried Chicken opened its first outlet in China in Beijing, near Tiananmen Square, the company mistranslated its slogan "Finger-lickin' Good" into Chinese characters that meant "eat your fingers off."

Material Girl

On March 11, 1989, PepsiCo, having paid $5 million to Madonna to promote Pepsi in four commercials, ran the first commercial—a wholesome, nostalgic two-minute video featuring the world premiere of the singer's new single, "Like a Prayer." The next day, Pepsi executives discovered that Madonna's actual "Like a Prayer" video, which had begun running on MTV, featured images of burning crosses, murder, and racism. When religious groups called for a boycott of Pepsi products, PepsiCo broke the contract with Madonna and ceased running the commercial. Madonna was allowed to keep the $5 million without filming any more commercials for Pepsi, and the controversy catapulted the single and the album to No. 1 on the *Billboard* charts.

Unidentified Flying Button

A photograph of an alleged UFO taken by an airline pilot over Venezuela in 1965 fooled experts for six years—until an engineer in Caracas admitted that he had taken a photograph of a button, placed it over an aerial shot, rephotographed it, and burned in a shadow of the "UFO" during processing.

A Crabby Response

In 1981, Chicago suburbanite Susan Benjamin wrote a letter to President Ronald Reagan to protest proposed cuts in federal education aid for handicapped children. In response, the White House sent her a form letter thanking her for her volunteer efforts, two glossy photographs (one of the president, the other of the first couple), and four recipe cards, including one for crabmeat casserole. Benjamin calculated the cost of making the seafood dish to be around $20, well beyond the financial reach of most Americans. The negative media attention prompted the woman in charge of answering the Reagans' mail to telephone Benjamin and apologize, and to avoid any further embarrassment the correspondence unit of the White

House substituted for the crabmeat recipe a less objectionable recipe for macaroni and cheese.

Fiddlesticks

On September 23, 1964, drama critic Walter Kerr, writing in the *New York Herald Tribune*, panned a new Broadway musical. "*Fiddler on the Roof* takes place in Anatevka, a village in Russia," wrote Kerr, "and I think it might be an altogether charming musical if only the people of Anatevka did not pause every now and again to give their regards to Broadway, with remembrance to Herald Square." *Fiddler on the Roof* ran for eight years, becoming one of the longest-running musicals on Broadway.

Child's Play

In November 2010, Amazon.com made the self-published *Pedophile's Guide to Love and Pleasure: A Child-Lover's Code of Conduct* by Philip Greaves available for purchase as an electronic book on its Web site. When news of the publication made headlines in the press, Amazon.com, whose guidelines forbid "pornography and hardcore material that depicts graphic sexual acts," defended its decision to sell the guide for pedophiles on grounds of free speech: "Amazon believes it is censorship not to sell certain titles because we believe their message is objectionable." When irate consumers launched two Facebook pages and a Twitter campaign calling for a boycott of the online retailer, Amazon reversed course and pulled the book from its Web site on November 11—but not before the publicity had catapulted the sales rankings of the controversial book in Amazon's Kindle store from No. 58,221 to No. 96. On December 20, police arrested Greaves in Pueblo, Colorado, and extradited him to Polk County, Florida, to face charges of distributing obscene material. Detectives in Winter Haven, Florida, had ordered an autographed copy of the book from Greaves, and when it arrived, obtained an arrest warrant.

Dr. Death Wish

On November 22, 1998, *60 Minutes* aired a videotaped recording made and supplied by euthanasia advocate Dr. Jack Kevorkian that showed him administering a lethal injection of potassium chloride to Thomas Youk, a man fatally ill with Lou Gehrig's disease. Kevorkian claimed that he had assisted 130 terminally ill people to self-administer lethal drugs to take their own lives. On April 13, 1999, Oakland County Circuit Court in Michigan sentenced Kevorkian, convicted of second-degree murder, to ten to twenty-five years in a maximum security prison.

Sting Operation

In 1956, Brazilian geneticist Warwick Kerr imported sixty-three killer bee queens from Africa to São Paulo in hopes of crossbreeding them with Brazilian bees to create more prolific honey producers. The following year, twenty-six killer bee queens and their swarms escaped from Kerr's laboratory and reproduced in the wild, spreading across South America and reaching into Mexico and the United States.

Aryan Physics

German dictator Adolf Hitler referred to atomic research as "Jewish physics" and banned its study from German universities. Hitler's anti-Semitic policies prompted Jewish physicists Albert Einstein, Edward Teller, Lise Meitner, and Leo Szilard to emigrate to the United States—where they helped develop the atomic bomb.

Oh Brother

On August 5, 1995, Hussein Kamel al-Majid, one of the most powerful men in the Iraqi government, and his younger brother Saddam, former head of the Iraqi Republican Guard, defected from Iraq to Jordan with their wives—Saddam Hussein's daughters, Raghad and Rana—and children. Debriefed by the CIA and MI6, they divulged extensive secrets regarding Iraq's chemical and biological weapons program. Six months later, Saddam Hussein sent a message to his sons-in-law, telling them if they returned to Iraq he would forgive their trespasses. Homesick for their country and former positions of power, Hussein Kamel al-Majid and Saddam Kamel al-Majid jumped at the opportunity. When the Kamel brothers and their families returned to Iraq, Saddam Hussein forgave his two daughters and grandchildren—and then put his two sons-in-law to death.

Intimate Knowledge

On January 10, 1989, the *Washington Post* reported that Jennifer Fitzgerald, a suspected presidential mistress, had "served President-elect Bush in a variety of positions."

Just What the Doctor Ordered

In 1685, when English king Charles II fell ill with kidney disease, doctors detrimentally let blood, unnecessarily cut off his hair, pointlessly applied blistering agents to his scalp, and put plasters of pitch and pigeon dung on the bottoms of his feet. They inflicted further harm by blowing the herb hellebore up his nose to make him sneeze nonexistent humors from his brain and then had him drink antimony and sulfate of zinc to induce vomiting. The doctors then further weakened the king by giving him purgatives to cleanse his bowels and spirit of human skull to supposedly stop the convulsions. During this time they also administered a plethora of tonics, herbs, and drugs, and finally let another twelve ounces of his blood. After five days of this "treatment," King Charles II died.

The K Stands for Kwality

In the 1980s, Kmart stores in Gainesville, Florida, introduced their own brand of wine, Kmarto, featuring Kmarto Lambrusco and Kmarto Blanco. Priced at $1.97 a bottle, the wine flopped.

Judging a Book by Its Author

In 1979, struggling writer Chuck Ross retyped Jerzy Kosinski's 1968 novel *Steps* in manuscript form, changed the title, and submitted the manuscript to fourteen publishing houses and thirteen literary agents under the pseudonym Erik Demos as an experiment. All twenty-seven—including Random House, the book's original publisher—rejected the novel, which had received the National Book Award in 1969 for best work of fiction and sold more than 400,000 copies.

The Great Yogurt Conspiracy

In September 1972, police officers arrested two founders of the Federation of Feminist Women's Health Centers, Carol Downer and Colleen Wilson, at their Los Angeles Women's Self-Help Clinic and charged them with practicing medicine without a license. Downer had inserted yogurt into the vagina of a women's center staff member. At the trial, known as "the Great Yogurt Conspiracy," Downer argued that applying yogurt as a home remedy for an ordinary yeast infection is not practicing medicine. The jury found her not guilty.

Fork in the Road

Forks, usually made with only two tines, originated in Tuscany, Italy, in the eleventh century, but the clergy frowned upon their use, insisting that only human fingers—along with spoons and knives—should be used to eat God's bounty.

Cheesed Off

In 1991, Kraft USA introduced its "Ready to Roll" contest in Chicago and Houston, giving consumers the opportunity to win prizes including a $17,000 minivan, one hundred bicycles, five hundred skateboards, and eight thousand packages of cheese by matching game pieces found in packages of Kraft Singles with those printed in Sunday newspaper fliers. A printing error created millions of matches, and approximately ten thousand people claimed they had winning matches for the minivan. Kraft nullified the contest and announced its plan to give each grand-prize winner $250 and a chance to win one of four minivans in a drawing. The thousands of upset winners filed a class action lawsuit, winning a $10-million settlement from Kraft.

Stop and Ask for Directions

The 1968 motion picture *Krakatoa: East of Java*, starring Maximilian Schell, Brian Keith, and Sal Mineo, follows the SS *Batavia Queen* as it is engulfed by the huge tidal wave created by the 1883 eruption of the volcanic island of Krakatoa. The eruption was heard approximately three thousand miles away, created sea waves almost 130 feet high, and killed nearly 36,000 people on nearby islands. Oddly, the filmmakers mistitled their movie. Krakatoa lies west of Java. It is east of Sumatra.

It'll Grow on You

In the 1930s, farmers in the southern United States began planting kudzu, a fast-growing, deep-rooted Asian vine, to prevent soil erosion. While the nitrogen-fixing bacteria that live on kudzu roots help enrich the soil, the vine can grow up to sixty feet high and spreads so rapidly that it is virtually impossible to control— wreaking havoc on the farmland.

A Mickey Mouse Idea

In his 1815 book, *Histoire Naturelle des Animaux Sans Vertèbre*, botanist Chevalier de Lamarck (1744–1829), attempting to explain why many animals possess vestiges of organs or bodily appendages, insisted that chopping off the tails of mice and letting them breed would produce tailless mice. It doesn't.

Nestlé Not-So-Quik

In March 2010, when Greenpeace spoofed a Kit Kat bar commercial on YouTube to protest Nestlé's use of palm oil obtained from suppliers that destroy Indonesian rain forests (the habitat of endangered orangutans), Nestlé refused to address public concerns, instead lobbying YouTube to remove the video and then accusing Facebook posters of copyright infringement. Nestlé's combative approach provoked thousands of people to join the Nestlé's Facebook page and post comments of protest, attracting the attention of the mainstream media. In May, Nestlé agreed to work with the Forest Trust to ensure that its sourcing of palm oil does not contribute to illegal rain forest clearance.

The Menu at the Last Supper

Last Supper, a painting by Marcos Zapata (1710–1773) in the cathedral of Cuzco, Peru, portrays Jesus and his twelve disciples about to dine on an Inca delicacy—roast guinea pig—and drink glasses of Inca beer called *chicha*. Aside from the fact that neither roast guinea pig nor *chicha* was served in biblical times, Jesus and his disciples observed kosher dietary laws, and rodents, including the guinea pig, are not kosher. Also, the Last Supper took place during Passover, when drinking beer, a leavened product, is forbidden.

Lawrence Welk Goes Punk

In 1987, approximately ten thousand Lawrence Welk *Polka Party* compact discs were distributed to record stores, but the CDs were actually the mislabeled punk rock soundtrack to *Sid and Nancy*, the movie chronicling the life of the Sex Pistols' Sid Vicious.

At Full Tilt

In 1173, an unknown architect designed a ten-foot-thick foundation for the bell tower in the Italian town of Pisa, but when construction on the tower began in 1174, the ground shifted and the building started leaning. Construction was halted for a hundred years, and the tower was completed in 1350, with the top tier built out of line with the rest of the tower in a vain attempt to correct the tilt. Tilting an average of a quarter inch per year, the tower has shifted seventeen feet from the perpendicular.

In 1934, the Italian government pumped concrete under the base to stop further tilting, but that project actually sped it up. In 1982, the government spent $10.5 million in another attempt to stop the leaning. Eventually the tower will topple over, though predictions vary widely as to precisely when.

Leaning Towers of Bologna

The Leaning Tower of Pisa is not the only leaning tower in the world or even in Italy. Two towers built in 1488 in Bologna, Italy, standing less than twenty feet apart, lean in opposite directions. The Torre degli Asinelli, a 320-foot-tall tower in the center of the Piazza di Porta Ravegnana, leans seven and a half feet from the perpendicular. Its twin tower, the Torre degli Garisenda, tilts eleven feet in the opposite direction.

Mmm Mmm Good!

During the Prussian siege of France, in 1870, a scarcity of meat prompted Voisin, an upscale restaurant in Paris, to prepare a Christmas dinner using animals from the zoo and elsewhere. The menu included consommé of elephant, braised kangaroo, antelope pâté, cat, and rat.

They're Gonna Crucify Me

In March 1966, Beatle John Lennon, interviewed by columnist Maureen Cleave in the *London Evening Standard*, said, "Christianity will go. It will vanish and shrink. . . . We're more popular than Jesus now. I don't know which will go first—rock and roll or Christianity." Five months later, when Cleave's interview with Lennon was reprinted in the teen fanzine *Datebook*, the headline touted Lennon's claim that the Beatles were "bigger than Jesus Christ," inciting anti-Beatles demonstrations across the Bible Belt in the American South, where irate fans burned Beatles albums in bonfires. Thirty-five radio stations across America banned Beatles records. At a press conference in Chicago on August 12, Lennon formally apologized for his remark.

The Butterfly Ballot

For the presidential election held on November 7, 2000, Theresa LePore, election supervisor for Palm Beach County, Florida, designed a "butterfly" ballot, placing the names of the presidential candidates on both the left- and right-hand pages of the ballot with arrows pointing to the center holes, in violation of Florida law. Voters claimed the ballot was so confusing that they accidentally cast their votes for Reform Party candidate Pat Buchanan, rather than Democratic candidate Al Gore, resulting in some 3,000 votes for Buchanan. Consequently, Gore lost the state of Florida by 524 votes, giving Republican candidate George W. Bush Florida's 25 electoral votes and the presidency.

Something Fishy

In his 1906 book, *On Leprosy and Fish-Eating*, British surgeon Sir Jonathan Hutchinson insisted that eating bad fish causes leprosy. Hutchinson had clearly failed to keep up with medical advances. In 1865, French chemist Louis Pasteur had proven that germs spread from person to person cause infectious diseases, and in 1874, Norwegian bacteriologist Gerhard Hansen identified a bacterium, *Mycobacterium leprae*, as the cause of leprosy.

In Search of the Planet Vulcan

In December 1859, French mathematician Urbain Jean Joseph Le Verrier, who had accurately predicted the location of the planet Neptune in 1846, announced the discovery of another planet, Vulcan, based on irregularities in the orbit of the planet Mercury and the sighting of a possible planet between Mercury and Venus by an amateur astronomer. Although the Paris Observatory, which Le Verrier directed, could never confirm the existence of Vulcan, Le Verrier went to his grave convinced that the planet existed. The irregularities in Mercury's orbit were eventually explained by Einstein's theory of relativity: The sun's massive gravity affects Mercury's path through space. In the 1960s, television producer Gene Roddenberry, creator of the science fiction series *Star Trek*, gave the name Vulcan to the fictional home planet of the character Mr. Spock.

The Seat of the Universe

Ancient Hindus believed that the world was supported on the backs of four elephants standing on top of a giant turtle.

Out of the Question

On October 31, 1936, four days before the presidential election, the influential weekly magazine *The Literary Digest*, having mailed more than ten million questionnaires to names drawn from lists of automobile and telephone owners, announced that Republican candidate Alfred M. Landon would win the election with 370 electoral votes. Four days later, Franklin D. Roosevelt won by one of the most lopsided landslides in history, garnering 523 electoral votes to Landon's 8. Since most Americans did not own automobiles or have telephones in 1936, the poll had skewed to affluent voters, most of whom were Republicans. Within a year, the debacle caused *The Literary Digest*'s demise.

Caught with His Pants Down

In 1998, incoming House Speaker Bob Livingston of Louisiana, chairman of the House Appropriations Committee, harshly criticized President Bill Clinton for his extramarital affair with Monica Lewinsky. On December 18, Larry Flynt, the publisher of *Hustler* magazine, having offered up to $1 million to anyone who could document an affair with a member of Congress, announced that he would disclose details of four extramarital affairs by Livingston. The next day, Livingston confessed that he had been unfaithful to his wife, withdrew his name as a candidate for House Speaker, and announced that he would resign his seat in the House of Representatives.

Yippie! It's Santa Claus!

On December 4, 1968, Yippie leader Jerry Rubin showed up during a hearing of the House Un-American Activities Committee, in Washington, D.C., dressed in a Santa Claus suit and toting a toy gun. Rubin said the toy gun was for "self-defense" and claimed his costume was typical for the committee, which he described as "a total circus." Rubin was barred from the hearing. Resulting newspaper headlines announced: "HUAC Bars Santa Claus."

The Brains Behind
the Operation

In 1949, Portuguese neurosurgeon Antonio Egas Moniz received the Nobel Prize in medicine for originating the prefrontal lobotomy, a barbaric surgical procedure in which parts of the front of the brain are removed to correct severe personality disorders. American neurologist Walter Freeman and American neurosurgeon James Watts popularized the lobotomy (frequently performed with a rudimentary ice pick) and claimed that the operation—despite its dubious results—separated the prefrontal lobes ("the rational brain") from the thalamic brain ("the emotional brain"). By 1955, after more than fifty thousand people in the United States had received lobotomies, leaving them sluggish and lethargic, critics correctly labeled the irreversible operation "mutilation."

The Spy Who Screwed Up

In September 1914, during World War I, German spy Carl Hans Lody, based in Edinburgh, Scotland, learned from acquaintances of a troop train traveling through Carlisle, England, with the window blinds shut. He also learned that a soldier aboard one of those trains, when asked where he was from, replied "Russia." Unbeknownst to Lody, the blinds on the troop trains had been shut so the Scottish soldiers from Ross-shire (not "Russia") could sleep. Lody sent a telegram to his German superiors, informing them that large numbers of Russian troops had landed in Aberdeen, Scotland,

and were about to be sent to France. In response, the German army held back two divisions from the Battle of the Marne in case the Russians landed. An allied counterattack forced the Germans to retreat, halting their assault on Paris. Arrested on October 13, Lody became the first foreign spy in Britain to be executed for espionage during World War I. On November 6, 1914, he was shot in the Tower of London.

Bridge over Troubled Waters

In 1580, the Thames Water Authority in London licensed to Dutch engineer Pieter Morice the rights to operate a waterwheel under an arch of London Bridge for the next five hundred years to supply water to the city. In the nineteenth century, when London Bridge was replaced and no longer constricted the river's flow enough to power a waterwheel, the city awarded Morice's descendants $3,750 a year in compensation until the year 2080.

In Denial

On January 27, 1998, on the *Today* show, First Lady Hillary Rodham Clinton, denying that her husband had had a sexual affair with White House intern Monica Lewinsky, stated: "It's a vast right-wing conspiracy that has been conspiring against my husband since the day he announced for president."

Dead to the World

In July 1916, while recovering in an army field hospital from serious shrapnel wounds inflicted during the Battle of the Somme, British poet Robert Graves read his own obituary in the *London Times*.

The High-Definition Battle

In the mid-1990s, Sony and Toshiba developed two competing high-resolution formats for movies but decided to join forces, combining the best of both formats into something called digital versatile disc, better known as DVD. But in 2002, the two companies threw common sense to the wind and began competing against each other to dominate the market with two new, separate, incompatible high-definition disc standards. Sony developed Blu-ray. Toshiba created HD DVD. In 2008, Sony paid Warner Bros. Studios a reported $400 million to drop HD DVD in favor of Blu-ray, prompting Toshiba to cease developing and making HD DVD. Had Sony and Toshiba joined forces in 2002 and developed a single high-definition format (rather than sacrificing eight years' worth of potential sales), high-definition discs would dominate the marketplace today. Instead, DVDs outsell Blu-ray discs by roughly four to one (as of 2011), and streaming media and video on demand are poised to prevail.

Waste Is a Terrible
Thing to Mind

On June 16, 1999, when sanitation engineers at a water treatment facility in Los Angeles cycled the power off and on to conduct a Y2K readiness test, a valve defaulted to its open position, causing four million gallons of raw sewage to spill into Woodley Avenue Park in Encino.

Tony Baloney

On April 20, 2010, an explosion on the offshore oil rig Deepwater Horizon killed eleven British Petroleum workers and caused more than four million barrels of crude oil to gush into the Gulf of Mexico from a mile below the surface over a period of eighty-six days, creating the biggest marine oil spill in history. On May 30 (Day 41), BP's chief executive officer, Tony Hayward, apologized to Gulf Coast residents. "There's no one who wants this thing over more than I do," he said. "I'd like my life back." On June 19 (Day 61), Hayward took the day off to sail aboard his fifty-two-foot yacht at a prestigious yacht race around England's Isle of Wight, infuriating residents of the Gulf Coast and prompting the mayor of Louisiana's Grand Isle, David Camardelle, to dub him Tony Baloney.

Hooker Taints Love Canal

In 1942, the Hooker Chemicals & Plastics Corp. began dumping thousands of drums filled with chemical waste into Love Canal, near Niagara Falls, New York, sometimes burying them in the muddy banks. Eleven years later, after burying 21,000 tons of toxic waste, Hooker sold the sixteen-acre site to the Niagara Falls Board of Education for $1. In 1976, the chemicals, leaking from the corroded containers and including seven known carcinogens, began bubbling up into nearby backyards and basements. Miscarriages had increased 50 percent in the area, the number of birth defects had risen significantly, cancer rates had skyrocketed, and the value of the 1,200 homes built near the site plunged. In 1979, the United States government spent $101 million to fund cleanup efforts and evacuate more than one thousand homes, an elementary school, and an entire neighborhood. The Department of Justice sued Hooker, and sixteen years later, in 1995, the company's successor, Occidental Chemical Corporation, agreed to pay the government $129 million (including $28 million in interest) to cover the costs of the Love Canal incident.

Lowe Life

On July 17, 1988, 25-year-old actor Rob Lowe went to Atlanta to attend the Democratic National Convention, picked up 16-year-old Jan Parsons and her friend, 22-year-old hair salon receptionist Tara Siebert, at the Club Rio nightclub, and took them back to his hotel room at the Atlanta Hilton and Towers, where he videotaped their sexual exploits together. Parsons and Siebert stole the tape from the video camera and made a duplicate. When Parsons' mother discovered the tape, she filed a civil suit against the star. Lowe avoided criminal charges by agreeing to spend twenty hours speaking to inmates in his hometown of Dayton, Ohio, but the unseemly episode made the Hollywood brat packer too hot to handle for several years. "There's no way that you can know how embarrassing it was," Lowe told *People* magazine in 1990. "No matter what adjective I choose, it would be trivializing it."

Bungle in the Jungle

In the late 1960s, billionaire Daniel K. Ludwig bought a parcel of land the size of Connecticut along the Jari River in the Brazilian Amazon basin, determined to mill paper on the site. After having 35,000 workers clear the land and plant it with pine and eucalyptus trees, Ludwig sent enormous barges carrying a giant pulp mill and paper plant—too large to sail through the Panama Canal—from Japan around Africa to the site on the Amazon. After Ludwig spent an estimated $1 billion on the project, the jungle defeated him. Leaf cutter ants destroyed crops and supplies, workers contracted malaria and meningitis, and the soil failed to support the pine and eucalyptus trees.

Separating the Wheat from the Chaff

In 1928, during a crisis in Soviet wheat production, Russian agronomist Trofim Denisovich Lysenko (1898–1976) claimed that seeds exposed to dry conditions or cold would acquire a resistance to drought or cold weather, and future generations of the grain would genetically inherit these traits. As head of the Soviet Academy of Agricultural Sciences, Lysenko deemed any belief in conventional genetics an act of treason. In 1953, Lysenko was made the director of the Institute of Genetics of the USSR Academy of Sciences, and his predecessor, Nikolai Vavilov, was arrested and exiled to a labor camp in Siberia. The implementation of Lysenko's incorrect theory resulted in widespread crop failures and famine and set back Soviet genetic research for decades.

First Things First

On October 30, 1945, two months after World War II ended, General Leslie Groves, a member of the Joint Chiefs of Staff who had headed the Manhattan Project, cabled a message from Washington, D.C., to General Douglas MacArthur in Japan, ordering U.S. occupation forces to seize and destroy Japan's five atomic research cyclotrons, but only after all available technical and experimental data had been obtained from them. On November 24, MacArthur sent a cable to each of the nine Joint Chiefs of Staff, stating that the cyclotrons had been seized on November 20 and destruction had begun on November 24—without first procuring the data. Subordinate staff officers filed all nine copies of the message, never showing them to the Joint Chiefs of Staff, against detailed orders to the contrary. No one became aware of the problem until November 28, when MacArthur received a cable from the general staff requesting that one of the cyclotrons be shipped to the United States for examination.

The Christmas Tree That Ate Pittsburgh

On February 18, 2000, Warren Wynne of Pittsburgh, Pennsylvania, finally got around to taking down his Christmas tree. Too lazy to carry the tree downstairs to the curb for pickup, 31-year-old Wynne hurled the tree out the window of his sixth-floor apartment, hitting a power line and knocking out electricity for approximately four hundred customers.

Terrible at Names

In 1521, Portuguese explorer Ferdinand Magellan, having crossed the Pacific Ocean without encountering a storm, named it *Mar Pacifico*, meaning "peaceful sea." In actuality, the Pacific Ocean is home to some of the most destructive storms, tidal waves, and typhoons on earth.

Think Different

In the fall of 2000, computer science engineer Tony Fadell offered RealNetworks the opportunity to buy his newly designed MP3 player, which could be loaded with music using an easy-to-use content-delivery system. RealNetworks passed on the device, as did

Fadell's former employer Philips. But Steve Jobs, chief executive officer of Apple, jumped at the opportunity, and today Fadell's device is known as the iPod and his content-delivery system is called iTunes. As of 2010, Apple controlled approximately 80 percent of the digital music market and was valued at $300 billion.

A Magnetic Smile

Fifteenth-century physician Marcellus incorrectly insisted that magnets could be used to cure toothaches.

Sappy Ending

In 1987, D. D. Soejarto, a plant researcher from the University of Illinois, extracted a sap sample from an unfamiliar species of tree in the Malaysian rain forest. Years later, Soejarto developed a compound from the sap in his laboratory that seemed to inhibit HIV. In 1992, he returned to Malaysia to extract more sap—only to discover that the tree had been cut down for lumber.

Nice Tie

In the 1941 movie *The Maltese Falcon*, when actor Humphrey Bogart slaps actor Peter Lorre in the face, Lorre is wearing a polkadot tie. When Lorre turns back, his tie suddenly has stripes.

The Nuclear Plant
That Never Was

In 1973, Public Service Indiana estimated the proposed cost of constructing the Marble Hill nuclear power plant near Madison, Indiana, at $700 million. When public hearings on the project ended and the project was approved in September 1977, estimated construction costs had doubled to $1.4 billion. In the wake of a 1979 attempt to cover up construction defects, building of the Marble Hill plant slowed considerably, and by 1984, the half-finished project had cost $2.5 billion and would require an additional $5.2 billion to complete. Convinced that continuing with construction would bankrupt Public Service Indiana, Governor Robert Orr scrapped all plans to finish the nuclear power plant and the project was completely abandoned.

Out of Line

On July 22, 1962, NASA launched the $18.5-million *Mariner 1* space probe, an unmanned craft designed to orbit Venus. Four minutes after takeoff from Cape Canaveral, Florida, the rocket veered off course and mission control pushed the destruct button, destroying the craft. The resulting investigation revealed that the craft had gone off course because a computer program was missing a simple overbar (a character that resembles a hyphen).

Getting into Hot Chocolate

On January 16, 2006, in the wake of the devastation caused by Hurricane Katrina, New Orleans mayor Ray Nagin made a speech on Martin Luther King Day, calling on the African-American community to rebuild "a chocolate New Orleans." The next day Nagin, who is African American, apologized for his divisive remarks. "How do you make chocolate?" he asked. "You take dark chocolate, you mix it with white milk, and it becomes a delicious drink. That is the chocolate I am talking about."

Get a Grip

The 1716 book *Onania: Or, the Heinous Sin of Self-Pollution* claimed that masturbation leads to insanity. By 1764, eighty editions of the book had been published. In the first American textbook of psychiatry, published in 1812, Dr. Benjamin Rush, a signer of the Declaration of Independence, further perpetuated this myth by incorrectly claiming that masturbation causes "seminal weakness, impotence, dysury, tabes dorsalis, pulmonary consumption, dyspepsia, dimness of sight, vertigo, epilepsy, hypochondriasis, loss of memory, manalgia, fatuity, and death."

Squeaky Clean

On March 15, 1992, members of the Eclaireuses et Eclaireurs de France youth group, using steel brushes to clean graffiti from the

Mayrieres cave, near the village of Bruniquel, France, wiped away part of the 15,000-year-old bison paintings.

The Audacity of Hope

On May 9, 2008, at a campaign event in Beaverton, Oregon, Democratic presidential candidate Barack Obama said, "Over the last fifteen months we've traveled to every corner of the United States. I've now been in fifty-seven states. I think . . . one left to go."

Xerox Gets Copied

In 1973, long before the advent of Macintosh and Windows-based personal computers, Xerox invented the Alto, the world's first computer with a window-based graphical user interface, a mouse, Ethernet networking, and a WYSIWYG (what-you-see-is-what-you-get) text processor. Rather than launching the personal computer revolution, Xerox manufactured a thousand Alto computers for the computer-science research community and distributed another five hundred to universities, including Stanford, Carnegie Mellon, and MIT. In 1979, in exchange for the opportunity to buy 100,000 shares of Apple stock before the company went public, Xerox gave Apple cofounder Steve Jobs and several of his engineers a tour of its Palo Alto Research Center, demonstrating the Alto. In 1981, Xerox introduced its own personal computer, the Star, incorporating many of the Alto's features, but by then, Apple and IBM had taken the lead in sales. Apple incorporated many of the Alto's features into its 1983 Lisa computer and its 1984 Macintosh.

Pimping Burgers

In 1972, when McDonald's opened one of its fast-food restaurants on the Champs-Élysées in Paris, the name for the Big Mac was translated into French as *Gran Mac*. In French, *gran mac* means "master pimp."

On the Ball

When playwright Arthur Miller took actress Marilyn Monroe to meet his parents, they fed her two bowls of matzah-ball soup. When she declined a third bowl, Miller's father asked her if she liked the soup. "Oh, I just love it," Monroe replied. "But gee, isn't there any other part of the matzah you can eat?"

A Big Hit with His Wife

On April 13, 1979, during the second round of the Masters golf tournament, professional golfer Mac McLendon drove his first ball into the crowd, hitting his wife, Joan, just below the shoulder and knocking her unconscious.

The Spy Who . . . What?

In the United States, the word *shag* is far less offensive than in other English-speaking countries, where the word is slang for "fornicate." In Singapore, authorities forced a movie distributor to change the title of the film *Austin Powers: The Spy Who Shagged Me* to *Austin Powers: The Spy Who Shoiked Me.* In the local Singlish dialect, the word *shoik* means "to speak well of."

That Sinking Feeling

In 1325, the Aztecs built their capital city, known as Tenochtitlan, on an island in the middle of Lake Texcoco, in the Valley of Mexico—on top of an underground reservoir of water. After conquering the Aztecs in 1521 and changing the name of the capital to Mexico City, Spanish colonizers continued using the underground reservoir, drained by wells for residents. As of 2010, Mexico City, with more than twenty million people, has been sinking at the rate of six to eight inches a year.

It's a Dog's Life

Millie, the Bush family dog, earned more money from book sales in 1991 than President George H. W. Bush did. The best-selling *Millie's Book*, written by First Lady Barbara Bush on behalf of the dog, earned $889,176 in royalties that year. During that same time period, Mr. Bush's book *Looking Forward*, published in 1987, earned $2,718 in royalties.

Taking the Bull by the Horns

In the Book of Exodus in the Hebrew Bible, when Moses comes down from Mount Sinai with the tablets containing the Ten Commandments, he has "rays of light" shining from his forehead. In the second century CE, when Aquila Ponticus translated the Hebrew Bible into Greek, he mistook the Hebrew word *karan* (meaning "rays of light") for *keren* (meaning "horns"), so that in the Greek Bible, Moses has "horns" emanating from his head when he descends from Mount Sinai. This mistranslation gave birth to the ridiculous belief that Jews have horns because they are in league with the devil, fanning the flames of anti-Semitism for centuries.

Lip Service

In 1989, Milli Vanilli accepted the Grammy Award for Best New Artist for their debut album, *Girl You Know It's True*, despite the fact that the duo—unemployed models Rob Pilatus and Fab Morvan—had merely lip-synched to songs recorded by studio musicians in music videos and on a concert tour. When Pilatus and Morvan demanded that they be allowed to sing on their second album, producer Frank Farian held a press conference on November 4, 1990, and revealed the truth, prompting the National Academy of Recording Arts and Sciences to revoke the Grammy Award.

Bad Trade

In 1960, college dropout and former marine Thomas Monaghan borrowed $900, bought DomiNick's, a failed pizza parlor in Ypsilanti, Michigan, and ran the business with his brother James. A year later, James traded his half of the company for his brother's second-hand Volkswagen Beetle. In 1965, Thomas Monaghan renamed his company Domino's Pizza. He sold it in 1998 for an estimated $1 billion.

The Argentine Firecracker

At two a.m. on October 7, 1974, U.S. Park Police patrolling the Tidal Basin, in Washington, D.C., pulled over intoxicated congressman Wilbur Mills of Arkansas for speeding. Mills's mistress, stripper Annabell Battistella (better known by the stage name Fanne Foxe, the "Argentine firecracker") jumped out of the car and dove into the nearby Tidal Basin, where she had to be rescued by Park Police. Two months later, a nationally humiliated Mills resigned as chairman of the House Ways and Means Committee and announced that he would not seek reelection in 1976.

Stewed Cabbage

Ancient Egyptians built temples to honor cabbage, and they believed that eating the vegetable prevented drunkenness. It doesn't.

Electing an Ass to Office

In September 1938, the citizens of Milton, Washington, elected Boston Curtis as their new Republican precinct committeeman by a fifty-one-vote plurality. Mayor Kenneth Simmons, a Democrat, had put Boston Curtis on the ballot, signing the filing notice as legal witness, to prove that many voters cast their vote carelessly. Boston Curtis was a brown mule.

Wardrobe Malfunction

On February 1, 2004, at the end of a flirtatious duet between Justin Timberlake and Janet Jackson to conclude the live Super Bowl half-time show, Timberlake sang the line "Gonna have you naked by the end of this song," reached over and pulled off a part of Jackson's bustier, and exposed Jackson's right breast to 140 million viewers for nine-sixteenths of a second. CBS quickly cut away while a seemingly stunned Jackson tried to cover her breast. The network received complaints from more than 542,000 people. "I am sorry that anyone was offended by the wardrobe malfunction during the half-time performance of the Super Bowl," Timberlake said afterward in an issued statement. "It was not intentional and is regrettable." The Federal Communications Commission fined CBS $550 million for the "deplorable stunt," and the phrase "wardrobe malfunction" entered the American lexicon.

N Stands for Nonexistent

In 1903, shortly after German physicist Wilhelm Conrad Röntgen discovered X-rays, French physicist René Blondlot claimed to have discovered a new type of radiation that he called N-rays, after Nancy-Université, where he had conducted his research. The following year, American physicist Robert Wood proved that Blondlot had misinterpreted his test results and that N-rays did not exist.

Mission Unaccomplished

In the 1986 movie *The Mission*, which takes place in the rain forest of Argentina in 1750, actor Robert De Niro stars as Spanish priest Rodrigo Mendoza, yet he speaks with a Brooklyn accent.

The Dark Side of Newton

British scientist Sir Isaac Newton (1642–1727), best remembered for discovering gravity and founding modern-day physics, toiled for three years to validate alchemy by transmuting one element into another, ideally a base metal into gold. Newton believed it was possible to prompt metals to ripen into new metals in a flask. It is not. Humans can transform one element into another only with the use of a particle accelerator—a device that wouldn't be invented until the twentieth century.

Seeing Russia

When asked in an interview conducted on September 11, 2008, by ABC's *World News* anchor Charlie Gibson to explain how Alaska's proximity to Russia gave her foreign affairs experience, Alaska governor and Republican vice presidential candidate Sarah Palin replied, "They're our next-door neighbors and you can actually see Russia from land here in Alaska, from an island in Alaska." Two days later, on *Saturday Night Live*, comedian Tina Fey, doing an impression of Palin, said, "I can see Russia from my house"—coining a popular catchphrase that further damaged Palin's credibility. Most Americans attributed Fey's comedic line to Palin, even though the governor never said it.

The Fertility Clause

Under a treaty signed on July 17, 1918, between France and Monaco, if Monaco's ruling House of Grimaldi should ever be without an heir, the country loses its independence and becomes a self-governing French protectorate.

Bombs Away

In 1994, the United States Postal Service produced a sheet of stamps commemorating the fiftieth anniversary of World War II, including a stamp depicting a mushroom cloud over Hiroshima. The resulting protest from the government of Japan prompted the Postal Service to nuke the stamp.

The Nutty Professor

On May 2, 1997, comedian Eddie Murphy, driving alone along Santa Monica Boulevard in West Hollywood while his wife and children were out of town, picked up twenty-year-old transvestite prostitute Atisone Seiuli. Soon after Seiuli got into the car, police pulled over Murphy and arrested Seiuli on an outstanding warrant. The police said Murphy had not done anything unlawful. Murphy claimed he was merely giving Seiuli a ride and that he frequently picked up prostitutes, gave them money, and told them to get off the street. "I was being a Good Samaritan," he told police.

Later that month, the *National Enquirer* ran an article titled "Eddie Murphy's Secret Life: His Transvestite Hooker Tells All." Incensed, Murphy filed a $5-million libel lawsuit against the *Enquirer*, but in July he dropped the suit and agreed to reimburse the tabloid's legal fees, convinced there had been no intended malice.

That's Easy for You to Say

A Matter of Perspective

"I haven't committed a crime. What I did was fail to comply with the law."

—NEW YORK CITY MAYOR
DAVID DINKINS

Come On Over Baby

"So, where's the Cannes Film Festival being held this year?"

—POP SINGER CHRISTINA AGUILERA

A Stroke of Genius

"The word 'genius' isn't applicable in football. A genius is a guy like Norman Einstein."

—FORMER WASHINGTON REDSKINS
QUARTERBACK JOE THEISMANN

Going On Forever

"I would not live forever, because we should not live forever, because if we were supposed to live forever, then we would live forever, but we cannot live forever, which is why I would not live forever."

—HEATHER WHITESTONE,
MISS ALABAMA 1994

Origin of the Species

"I'm not anorexic. I'm from Texas."

—POP SINGER JESSICA SIMPSON

Talking in Circles

"We're going to turn this team around 360 degrees."

—DALLAS MAVERICKS BASKETBALL
PLAYER JASON KIDD

Put That in Your Pipe

"Smoking kills. If you're killed, you've lost a very important part of your life."

—ACTRESS BROOKE SHIELDS

Clearing the Air

"We have to pause and ask ourselves: 'How much clean air do we need?'"

—CHRYSLER CHAIRMAN LEE IACOCCA

From Russia, with Love

To save money in the 1970s, the United States Department of State hired Soviet construction workers to build a new U.S. embassy in Moscow. The State Department, expecting the Soviets to plant listening devices in the building, planned to remove them upon taking control of the building. When the eight-story multimillion-dollar building was completed in 1985, U.S. security experts detected thousands of electronic diodes mixed into the concrete and hundreds of tiny microphones with their wires hidden inside steel beams and reinforcing rods. Rather than dismantling the building to find all the bugs, Congress budgeted $240 million to build a new one—this time, without Soviet construction workers.

The Sky Is Falling

On March 12, 1998, a headline on the front page of the *New York Times* declared: "Asteroid Is Expected to Make a Pass Close to Earth in 2028." Astronomer Brian G. Marsden, director of the Central Bureau for Astronomical Telegrams at the Smithsonian Astrophysical Observatory in Cambridge, Massachusetts, predicted that an asteroid roughly a mile in diameter and known as 1997 XF11 would pass within 30,000 miles of earth on October 26, 2028, at a speed of 4,500 miles per hour and might hit our planet. Later that same day, astronomers Dr. Donald K. Yeomans and Dr. Paul W. Chodas, at NASA's Jet Propulsion Laboratory, in Pasadena,

California, announced that 1997 XF11 would pass well beyond the moon's distance from earth with a zero probability of impacting the planet. Using photographs taken at Caltech's Palomar Observatory of 1997 XF11 on its previous pass in 1990 and Marsden's new data, the scientists calculated that the asteroid would "pass at a rather comfortable distance of about 600,000 miles."

Blowing the Election

In the spring of 1902, when the volcano Mount Pelée on the island of Martinique threatened to erupt, Governor Louis Mouttet refused to allow the residents of the town of Saint-Pierre to evacuate because important elections were scheduled to take place on May 11. Three days before the election, the volcano erupted, destroying the town and killing approximately 28,000 people in two minutes. Mouttet and his wife, having fled Saint-Pierre a few hours before the eruption, were buried in a lava flow.

Headstrong Harry

In 1980, when Mount Saint Helens, a volcano in the Cascade Mountains south of Seattle, threatened to erupt, the government evacuated three hundred loggers, fifty forest rangers and their families, and sixty residents of the tiny village of Spirit Lake. One defiant resident, 84-year-old Harry Truman, operator of the Mount Saint Helens Lodge, located less than two miles from the crater, refused to leave. Said Truman, "That mountain just doesn't dare blow up on me." The volcano erupted on May 18, 1980, with a blast five hundred times more powerful than the atomic bomb on Hiroshima, blowing the entire top off Mount Saint Helens and killing sixty people, including Harry Truman and his sixteen cats.

Cancel the Engagement

In 1993, General Carl Mundy Jr., determined to reduce the number of failed marriages among marines, announced that as of September 30, 1995, the Marine Corps would no longer accept married recruits—despite the fact that only 5 percent of marines were married. Mundy, however, had failed to first consult with Defense Secretary Les Aspin or President Bill Clinton before declaring the policy. To quell the resulting public outcry, Aspin swiftly canceled the policy.

Cosmic Gilligan

When a meteorite hits Gilligan's Island in an episode of the 1960s sitcom, the Professor, after measuring the meteorite's radiation with a bamboo Geiger counter, claims: "There were cosmic rays, which aren't as deadly as interstellar radiation; however, they can kill you." The Professor is just plain wrong. Cosmic rays are a form of radiation that is far too weak to endanger anyone.

The Game's Up

On November 17, 1968, when the New York Jets were beating the Oakland Raiders by three points with less than a minute left in the game, NBC switched from its coverage of the game to its scheduled broadcast of the movie *Heidi*. In the final fifty seconds, the Raiders scored two touchdowns, winning the game 43–32.

Not Even Close

In the October 31, 1977, issue of *New York* magazine, business reporter Bill Flanagan predicted that the Steven Spielberg movie *Close Encounters of the Third Kind* would be "a colossal flop," insisting that the film "lacks dazzle, charm, wit, and imagination" and sending Columbia Pictures stock into a tailspin. *Close Encounters* became one of Columbia Pictures' most profitable films ever.

Testament to Overstatement

In the New Testament, Jesus says, "You have heard that it was said, 'You shall love your neighbor and hate your enemy'" (Matthew 5:43). While the commandment "Love thy neighbor as thyself" appears in Leviticus 19:18, the commandment "hate thy enemy" does not appear in the Hebrew Bible or any Rabbinic literature.

Titanic Blunder

On April 15, 1912, the headline on the front page of the *New York Evening Sun* announced, "All Saved from *Titanic* After Collision," and the accompanying article reported that the SS *Carpathia* and SS *Parisian* had rescued the damaged ocean liner and were towing it to Halifax, Nova Scotia. Reporters had misinterpreted garbled telegraph messages. The *Titanic* sank on April 15, and the *Carpathia* rescued 705 passengers. The other 1,523 passengers were killed.

There Goes the Neighborhood

In 1985, the Virginia chapter of the Ku Klux Klan unseated Jordan Gollub as its grand dragon after discovering that he was Jewish. Four years later, a Mississippi chapter of the Ku Klux Klan discovered that their grand dragon was Jewish. His name? Jordan Gollub.

The Piltdown Chicken

On October 15, 1999, the National Geographic Society unveiled a recently discovered 125-million-year-old fossil smuggled out of China that showed a birdlike creature with the tail of a carnivorous dinosaur, dubbed *Archaeoraptor liaoningensis*, proving that birds evolved from dinosaurs. The Society described the remarkable fossil in the November 1999 issue of its magazine. When Chinese scientist Xu Xing discerned that *A. liaoningensis* was merely a composite of fossils from two different creatures, *U.S. News & World Report* dubbed the invented creature the Piltdown Chicken.

Dead Wrong

In June 1897, London newspapers, discovering that a man named Clemens had fallen ill at the London address where novelist Samuel Clemens (better known as Mark Twain) was living, reported that Twain (rather than his cousin James Ross Clemens) was ailing. Twain, working in seclusion in London and mourning the recent death of his eldest daughter, received a visit from *New York Journal* correspondent Frank Marshall White, who had been instructed by two telegrams from his editor to investigate whether Twain was dying in poverty or had already died in poverty. Twain replied: "The report of my death was an exaggeration."

Keep Your Shirt On

In 1816, poet and playwright Samuel Coleridge heard his death mentioned in a London hotel by a man reading a newspaper report aloud. When Coleridge asked to see the paper, the man remarked how odd it was that Coleridge had hung himself in the wake of his successful play *Remorse*, but noted that the poet was "a strange mad fellow." Coleridge replied: "Indeed, sir, it is a most extraordinary thing that he should have hanged himself, be the subject of an inquest, and yet that he should at this moment be speaking to you." Authorities had identified the dead body cut down from a tree in

Hyde Park by a marking on his shirt that read "S. T. Coleridge." Coleridge speculated that the shirt had been stolen from him.

Tinkle, Tinkle Little Star

On September 8, 1992, Lieutenant Colonel Don Snelgrove crashed the $18-million F-16 Air Force jet he was piloting. The U.S. Air Force determined, after a one-year investigation, that Snelgrove had crashed because he was distracted while trying to urinate in his plastic "piddle pack."

Snow Blind

In 1611, German mathematician and astronomer Johannes Kepler wrote a treatise titled *The Six-Cornered Snowflake* to explain why all snowflakes have a hexagonal symmetry. In his thirty-page essay, he was unable to offer an answer.

Fool on the Hill

On September 17, 2002, during a speech in Nashville, Tennessee, President George W. Bush said, "There's an old saying in Tennessee—I know it's in Texas, probably in Tennessee—that says, fool me once, shame on . . . shame on you. Fool me . . . you can't get fooled again."

Diary of a Madman

In 1983, the German magazine *Stern* paid nearly $4 million to acquire sixty-two volumes of Adolf Hitler's secret handwritten diaries, allegedly found by farmers in the wreckage of a cargo plane near Dresden, Germany, nine days before Hitler's death in 1945. After historians Hugh Trevor-Roper and Gerhard Weinberg authenticated the diaries, *Newsweek* and the *Sunday Times* bought the rights to publish the diaries. But handwriting experts concluded that the diaries were forgeries, and further investigation revealed that the paper contained polyester fibers, invented after World War II—destroying *Stern's* credibility. Konrad Kujau, a German forger living in Stuttgart, had forged the diaries and sold them to *Stern*. In 1985, Kujau was sentenced to forty-two months in prison. *Stern* never recovered the $4 million.

The Heat Is On

Until the late 1700s, many scientists believed that heat is an invisible fluid called "caloric." They insisted that an object becomes warm when caloric flows into it and grows cold when caloric flows out of it. Since an object weighs the same whether it is hot or cold, scientists believed that caloric was weightless and could not be considered matter.

I'd Rather Be Kipling

On May 7, 1995, the *New York Times* identified Kafiristan as an imaginary place invented by novelist Rudyard Kipling. Kafiristan is the former name of a region in northeastern Afghanistan.

Mistaken Identity

On September 30, 2000, the *New York Times* published an Associated Press photograph of an Israeli soldier holding a bully club who appeared to be victimizing a young man with a bleeding head. The caption read: "Israeli soldier and Palestinian on the Temple Mount." The young man was actually Tuvia Grossman, a Jewish student from Chicago. A mob of Palestinian Arabs had pulled him and two of his friends from a taxicab in the Arab neighborhood of Wadi al-Joz (not the Old City, where the Temple Mount is located) and severely beaten and stabbed them. The Israeli soldier was holding his bully club to protect Grossman from the mob. The photograph also showed a gas station behind the soldier. There are no gas stations on the Temple Mount.

The Unreal Thing

In 1985, Pepsi-Cola, advertised as "The Choice of a New Generation" in television commercials starring Michael Jackson, began outselling Coca-Cola in supermarkets. Executives at the Coca-Cola Company decided to counter this challenge by reformulating the well-loved Coca-Cola for the first time in ninety-nine years. The company launched New Coke on April 23. The public hated it. Less than three months later, the Coca-Cola Company resurrected old Coke as Coca-Cola Classic. New Coke fizzled away, remembered as the marketing fiasco of the decade.

Now That's a Stretch

In July 1973, a Senate committee investigating the 1972 Watergate break-in learned that President Richard M. Nixon, who insisted that he took no part in the break-in or the subsequent cover-up, had secretly made tape recordings of conversations in the Oval Office. When the House of Representatives initiated steps to impeach him, the president handed over the tapes to United States District Court Judge John J. Sirica—with three key conversations erased, including a crucial eighteen-and-a-half-minute section that Nixon claimed had been accidentally erased by his secretary, Rose Mary Woods, while she was transcribing the tapes. Woods posed for photographs in her office to show how she might have accidentally erased part of the tape by reaching far back over her left shoulder for a telephone while her right foot remained pressing a pedal that controlled the transcription machine. The controversy forced Nixon to release additional transcripts of the tapes, revealing that he had apparently authorized the Watergate cover-up. On August 9, having lost almost all of his support in Congress, Nixon resigned. In his televised interviews with talk show host David Frost in 1976, Nixon admitted that his biggest mistake was failing to destroy the tapes.

Rocket's Red Glare

On January 13, 1920, the *New York Times* editorialized that rocket scientist Robert H. Goddard "does not know the relation of action to reaction, and of the need to have something better than a vacuum against which to react—to say that would be absurd. Of course he only seems to lack the knowledge ladled out daily in high schools." Five years later, Goddard launched the first liquid-fuel rocket. On July 17, 1969, three days before the *Apollo 11* astronauts landed on the moon, the *New York Times* retracted the statement.

Flee the Unfriendly Skies

On August 10, 2010, when Jet-Blue flight 1052 landed at New York's John F. Kennedy International Airport, flight attendant Steven Slater, an exasperated and slightly intoxicated twenty-year veteran of the airline industry, cursed at the passengers over the plane's public address system, announced his resignation, grabbed a couple of beers from the galley, and slid down the inflated emergency chute that he had deployed. Police arrested Slater at his home in Queens and charged him with felony criminal mischief and reckless endangerment. Fined $10,000 to help replace the chute, Slater agreed to undergo counseling for one year.

In Space No One Can Hear You Scribble

During the space race in the 1960s, NASA spent $1 million to develop a ballpoint pen that would write in zero gravity. The Soviet Union solved the same problem by giving their cosmonauts pencils.

Up to Bat

On January 20, 1982, as British heavy metal rock star Ozzy Osbourne, a former member of the group Black Sabbath, performed at the Veterans Memorial Auditorium in Des Moines, Iowa, a fan threw a bat on stage. Osbourne, convinced that the bat was a rubber toy, bit its head off. Immediately after the concert, Osbourne sought medical treatment at two hospitals and received a rabies shot, a rabies vaccine, and a tetanus shot.

Stealing the Show

On September 27, 2004, NBC announced that Jay Leno, host of *The Tonight Show*, would step down in May 2009, at which time Conan O'Brien would take over as host of the show. Five years later, NBC network president Jeff Zucker announced that Leno would host his own prime-time, one-hour talk show at ten p.m. each weeknight. The resulting plunge in viewership and advertising revenue of both

The Jay Leno Show and *The Tonight Show with Conan O'Brien* prompted the network to return *The Tonight Show* to Leno in March 2010, after paying $33 million to O'Brien to leave the show. Eight months later, O'Brien returned to late-night television on the cable channel TBS.

There's No Place Like Nome

Around 1850, a British naval officer wrote "? Name" on a diagram of the unidentified cape his ship was sailing past in Alaska. A cartographer copying the map misinterpreted the question mark in the notation as the letter *C*, an abbreviation for "Cape," and read the letter *a* in "Name" as an *o*, dubbing the spot Cape Nome.

The Beatles Meet the Crickets

John Lennon and Stuart Sutcliffe named their band the Beatles, changing the second letter *e* to *a*, to give the word a double meaning—inspired by the way the name of Buddy Holly's band, the Crickets, played off cricket the game and cricket the insect. After achieving worldwide fame, the Beatles met the Crickets, who had no idea that cricket is a game in England.

The Flip-Flopper

On March 16, 2004, during an appearance at Marshall University, in Huntington, West Virginia, Democratic presidential candidate

John Kerry tried to explain that he had voted for an early version of a bill to allocate an additional $87 billion for the wars in Iraq and Afghanistan but later voted against the final version of the bill. "I actually did vote for the $87 billion before I voted against it," he said. When Kerry won the Democratic presidential nomination, the Bush campaign used Kerry's botched remark as the focal point of a multimillion-dollar advertising campaign to paint the Massachusetts senator as a flip-flopper. Republican strategist Karl Rove called the statement "the gift that keeps on giving."

For Your Convenience

In April 1994, the NYNEX telephone company sent a mailing to three million of its calling-card customers in New York to promote a sweepstakes, accidentally printing each cardholder's secret personal identification number (PIN) on the outside of the mailer—for anyone to see.

A Tale of the Tub

On December 28, 1917, the *New York Evening Mail* published an article titled "A Neglected Anniversary" by American journalist H. L. Mencken. In the article, Mencken reported the history of the bathtub, claiming that the bathtub had not been introduced into the United States until 1842 and was initially opposed, until President Millard Fillmore had a bathtub installed in the White House in 1850. The story was widely reported and continues to be retold in books and magazines to this day. In 1926, Mencken revealed that his article was a hoax.

The Balloon Boy

On October 15, 2009, Richard and Mayumi Heene called the police to report that their homemade, UFO-shaped, silvery balloon filled with helium had accidentally come untethered in their backyard in Fort Collins, Colorado, and floated away with their six-year-old son, Falcon, who had climbed into a box compartment attached to the balloon. Over the next two hours, the balloon reached altitudes of seven thousand feet, traveled some fifty miles, attracted national media coverage, and ultimately landed gently near the Denver airport, where authorities shut down the airport and sent military helicopters to retrieve the boy.

Unable to locate Falcon, authorities launched a manhunt, ultimately discovering Falcon hiding in a cardboard box in the attic at home. In a live interview with CNN, Falcon said he had heard his family calling his name. When his father asked him why he didn't come out, Falcon replied, "You had said that we did this for a show." Sheriff Jim Alderden of Larimer County, calling the episode a hoax perpetrated to generate publicity for a reality TV show, pressed felony charges against the Heenes. Richard Heene served ninety days in jail and was fined $36,000. His wife, Mayumi, was sentenced to ten weekends of community service.

It Ain't Over Till I Say So

Japanese soldier Hiroo Onodo, stationed on the Philippine island of Lubang in 1944, refused to believe World War II had ended—dismissing dropped leaflets as propaganda, attempts by his family to contact him as impersonations, and stacks of Japanese newspapers left for him in the jungle as clever forgeries. In 1974, Onodo discovered a Japanese backpacker, Norio Suzuki, camping in the jungle and, convinced that Suzuki was an authentic Japanese, admitted that only a direct order from his commanding officer would convince him to leave the island. On March 9, Major Yoshimi Taniguchi arrived in Lubang and formally ordered the tenacious Onoda to cease fighting.

Earth to Iridium

In 1997, Iridium Communications promised crystal-clear cellular phone service anywhere on the planet and launched sixty-six satellites into orbit at a cost of $5 billion. With a $3,000 price tag for an Iridium satellite phone (that only worked outdoors) and international calling rates of up to $7 a minute, the company signed up a mere fifteen thousand customers before going bankrupt in 1999.

Inventive Diagnosis

In the 1850s, the schoolmaster of a one-room schoolhouse in Port Huron, Michigan, diagnosed third-grader Thomas Edison with mental retardation and expelled him from school. Edison—who went on to invent the lightbulb, the phonograph, and the movie projector—was actually partially deaf, the result of a bout with scarlet fever.

Phony Embryos

German biologist Ernst Haeckel (1834–1919) insisted that a human embryo goes through the same stages of mankind's evolution, coining the phrase "ontogeny recapitulates phylogeny" to describe this process. Haeckel published drawings to support this incorrect claim and to prove his questionable theory that the more closely two animals resemble each other (such as humans and primates), the longer their embryos remain identical. In 1997, British embryologist Michael Richardson and his colleagues published photographs in the August issue of the journal *Anatomy and Embryology* comparing actual embryos with Haeckel's drawings, proving them fraudulent and deliberately misleading.

Psychic Investment Advice

In California in the early 1980s, Orange County elected officials, having created a huge budget deficit over several years, pressured county treasurer Robert Citron to invest $8 billion of the county's funds in high-risk securities known as derivatives. Based on interest rate predictions from a mail-order astrologer and a psychic, Citron's investments produced 35 percent of the county's locally generated revenue for a short time, but by December 1, 1994, Citron had lost $1.64 billion. On December 6, 1994, affluent Orange County, California, declared the largest municipal bankruptcy in history. Citron was fined $100,000 and served eight months in a work-release program.

Out of Thin Air

In the 1770s, French scientist Antoine-Laurent Lavoisier (1743–1794), convinced that his newly discovered gas was the active ingredient in all acids, inaccurately named the gas "oxygen" (Greek for "acid maker"). Oxygen is not essential to acidic properties.

Going Hog Wild

During colonial times, New Englanders, convinced that raw potatoes contained an aphrodisiac that induced behavior that shortened a person's life, fed potatoes to pigs as fodder—instead of taking advantage of an inexpensive and plentiful food.

A Nip in the Air

In 1978, to prevent employees from stealing the miniature liquor bottles served aboard flights, Pan Am secretly installed a gadget in the liquor cabinets aboard its planes to count the number of times the cabinet was opened. Stewardess Susan Becker, discovering one of the unfamiliar gadgets aboard an airborne Boeing 707 and thinking it might be a bomb, informed the pilot, who made an emergency

landing, instructing the eighty passengers to use the emergency
exits with the inflatable slides—at a cost of approximately $20,000.

What to Expect When You're Using a Pen

In Mexico, the advertising agency for the
Parker pen company mistranslated the
phrase "won't leak in your pocket and embar-
rass you" by incorrectly using the Spanish
word *embarazar*, which made the phrase
read, "won't leak in your pocket and make you pregnant."

Have a Nice Weekend

In 1941, U.S. naval intelligence, having broken the Japanese code,
knew that Japan planned to attack the United States—but not
exactly where. On Saturday, December 6, 1941, Mrs. Dorothy Edg-
ers, working in the Office of Naval Intelligence, decoded an intercepted Japanese message that indicated that the target would be
Honolulu. Her superior officer, Lieutenant Commander Al Kramer,
told her the message needed more work and could wait until
Monday morning. The Japanese attacked Pearl Harbor on Sunday,
December 7, 1941.

The Fountain of Death

In 820 CE, Chinese herbal practitioner Liu Pi concocted an antiaging elixir and presented it to Emperor Hsien-tsung. The emperor drank the potion and died.

No Bones About It

In 1927, Canadian anatomy professor Davidson Black identified the 375,000-year-old fossils found at Zhoukoudian, near Beijing, as the partial remains of more than thirty prehistoric people, collectively known as the Peking Man. In December 1941, shortly after the Japanese attack on Pearl Harbor, the Japanese captured a group of American marines preparing to take the remains from Beijing to Tientsin for safekeeping. The Peking Man, one of the greatest anthropological-archaeological finds of modern times, has been missing ever since.

Deadly Translations

In 1965, the Pepsi slogan "Come Alive with the Pepsi Generation" was translated into Chinese for the Taiwanese as "Pepsi will bring your ancestors back from the dead." In Germany, the slogan read, "Come out of the grave with Pepsi."

How to Pick Up Chicks

In the 1970s, the advertising slogan for Perdue chicken, "It takes a strong man to make a tender chicken," created by advertising legend Ed McCabe, was purportedly translated into Spanish as "It takes an aroused man to make a chicken affectionate."

No Big Deal

In 1979, 23-year-old Bill Gates offered to sell his software company, Microsoft Corp., a twenty-eight-employee partnership valued at $2 million, to billionaire Ross Perot for somewhere between $6 and $15 million, but Perot balked at the price and turned down the opportunity. By 1992, when Perot ran for president of the United States, the stock market valued Microsoft at more than $21 billion, and Gates was the richest person in the United States.

Surgery Switcheroo

On the morning of March 13, 1980, surgeons mixed up Virginia Edmonson and Annie Robinson, two middle-aged women scheduled for surgery on the same day at Philadelphia's Graduate Hospital. Edmonson had checked in for spinal surgery but had a parathyroid gland removed from the front of her neck, and Robinson, who had come in to have her parathyroid problem treated, underwent surgery for a cervical laminectomy at the back of her head.

It's Not Rocket Science

On September 23, 1999, NASA lost contact with the $125-million *Mars Climate Orbiter* spacecraft, which was only sixty miles from its destination. Engineers at NASA's Jet Propulsion Laboratory had used metric measurements to guide the spacecraft. Lockheed Martin had engineered the *Orbiter* to be guided in imperial units of poundals.

Call of the Wild

Domino's Pizza had to change its first advertising slogan in the United Kingdom, "One call does it all." In the UK, a "call" refers to a personal visit from a call girl.

The Additive with Too Many Negatives

During the Arab oil embargo in the 1970s, American oil companies began adding MTBE (methyl tertiary-butyl ether) to gasoline to boost octane, help gasoline burn more efficiently, replace lead, and minimize air pollutants. Unfortunately, despite its many benefits, water-soluble MTBE tends to leak from underground storage tanks at gas stations, contaminates well water, and does not biodegrade easily, making it difficult and highly expensive to clean up once contamination occurs. Even fairly small amounts of MTBE can give water an unpleasant taste and odor. A 2001 study by the U.S.

Geological Survey found MTBE in 14 percent of all drinking water wells sampled in urban areas. Since then, many states have begun to limit or ban MTBE and government tax subsidies have encouraged a number of oil companies to replace the MTBE in their gasoline with ethanol.

Stand and Deliver

In December 1996, a Pizza Hut outlet in Kansas City, Missouri, refused to deliver $450 worth of pizza to the student honor luncheon at the Paseo Academy School of Fine and Performing Arts, claiming that the neighborhood was unsafe for its drivers. A few days later, unaware of the incident, the Kansas City Board of Education awarded Pizza Hut a $170,000 contract to deliver pizza to twenty-one schools in the city, including Paseo Academy. On January 22, 1997, having learned about the pizza redlining, the board of education canceled the contract.

Polish Your Furniture with Pee

SC Johnson introduced Pledge furniture polish as Pliz in the Netherlands, unaware that the Dutch pronunciation of the word sounds remarkably close to the Dutch word for "piss."

Fun with Nuclear Waste

Nuclear breeder reactors produce plutonium-239, a man-made radioisotope and one of the most toxic substances known to mankind. Used to make nuclear bombs, plutonium-239 has a half-life of 24,100 years, meaning the amount of emitted radioactivity decreases by half after 24,100 years. At that rate, it takes 240,000 years for plutonium-239 to be considered safe. Scientists have not found a permanent method of disposing of the radioisotope. The average nuclear power plant generates 30 tons of radioactive waste each year. As of April 2011, there were 439 nuclear reactors operating worldwide and another 62 under construction.

Small Potatoes

When Pope John Paul II visited Miami, a local T-shirt maker translated the phrase "I saw the pope" into Spanish by incorrectly using the feminine *la papa* instead of the masculine *el papa*, which made the T-shirts read: "I saw the potato."

Partly Cloudy with
a Chance of Armageddon

In 1919, seismologist and meteorologist Albert Porta resolutely declared, "The conjunction of six planets on December 17 could generate a magnetic current that might cause the sun to explode and engulf the earth."

A Breath of Fresh Air

English chemist Joseph Priestley (1733–1804) believed that anything that could burn contained a special substance called phlogiston. When the object was burned, phlogiston escaped into the atmosphere. In 1774, Priestley heated red oxide of mercury and red oxide of lead, captured the resulting gas, and found that a mouse would stay conscious twice as long in a sealed container of the gas as it would in a sealed container of air. Priestly called his new gas "dephlogisticated air." In reality, it was simply oxygen.

The Three Wise Men and Quetzalcoatl

On November 18, 1994, officials in San Jose, California, unveiled in Plaza de Cesar Chavez an eight-foot-tall statue of Quetzalcoatl, the feathered serpent god of ancient Mesoamerica—ignoring protests from offended Christians. Built with public funds at a cost of $500,000, the statue was meant to be a multicultural symbol honoring San Jose's Latino community. A federal district court had ruled that erecting pagan idols with tax dollars does not violate the separation between church and state—if people no longer worship the idol. Two weeks later, those same city officials ordered the removal of a privately funded Nativity scene from the annual Christmas display in the plaza to avoid offending non-Christian citizens. When city hall received thousands of phone calls protesting the removal of the

Nativity scene, San Jose officials agreed to return the crèche alongside the statue of Quetzalcoatl.

Smoke and Mirrors

In 1987, R.J. Reynolds Tobacco Company introduced Premier, advertised as the world's "cleanest cigarette." A smoker would light the carbon element at the tip of the cigarette and inhale, pulling the heated air through an aluminum cylinder filled with "flavor beads" and a pinch of tobacco, followed by a filter—to fill his or her lungs with hot air infused with nicotine. However, the carbon element was nearly impossible to light, sucking air through the cigarette was strenuous, and the heated, nicotine-infused air tasted vile. Four months later, R.J. Reynolds ceased making Premier, having lost an estimated $325 million on the harebrained scheme.

A Just-So Story

In the 1930s, a newspaper to which novelist Rudyard Kipling subscribed incorrectly announced his death. In a letter to the editor, Kipling wrote: "I've just read that I am dead. Don't forget to delete me from your list of subscribers."

Invasion of Piracy

In 1991, Procter & Gamble, determined to find out who leaked some of the company's proprietary information to the *Wall Street*

Journal, obtained a subpoena and the help of the Cincinnati police to examine the Cincinnati Bell phone records of some 800,000 people in the greater Cincinnati area. When the press, lawyers, and public denounced Procter & Gamble for invasion of privacy, the company swiftly ended its unconstitutional search. CEO Edwin L. Artzt sent a letter to employees apologizing for his "error of judgment," which "created a problem that was larger than the one we were trying to solve."

The Earth Is Flat

English inventor Samuel Birley Rowbotham (1816–1884), author of the book *Zetetic Astronomy: Earth Not a Globe* (written under the pseudonym Parallax), insisted that the earth is a flat disk centered at the North Pole and circumscribed by a wall of ice, with the sun, moon, planets, and stars only a few hundred miles above the earth's surface. Rowbotham founded the Zetetic Society in England and New York, attracting thousands of members and succeeded in 1956 by the International Flat Earth Society.

Do They Know It's Christmas?

In 1984, several pop and rock stars—including Bob Geldof, Phil Collins, Bono, Sting, George Michael, and Boy George—joined together as Band Aid and recorded a song to raise money to buy food and medical supplies for the victims of a widespread famine in Ethiopia. The resulting song, "Do They Know It's Christmas?"

written by Bob Geldof and Midge Ure, sold more than three million copies. Critics pointed out that the majority of people in Ethiopia are Muslims and animists and do not celebrate Christmas.

Eyes for Detail

In Alfred Hitchcock's 1960 horror film *Psycho*, the famous shower scene ends with an extreme close-up of Janet Leigh's eye, with her pupil tightly contracted. When people die, their pupils dilate.

Down to Earth

In 150 CE, Greek astronomer Ptolemy wrote *The Almagest*, in which he claimed that the sun, moon, and planets rotate around the earth, which is motionless and located at the center of the universe. Ptolemy also insisted that the earth does not move because otherwise people, animals, and objects would be thrown into the air. He also believed that the stars are merely bright spots of light fixed within a concave dome that arches over the universe. These theories were accepted as fact for the next 1,500 years.

Is There a Real Doctor in the House?

The influential ancient Greek physician Galen (circa 130–200 CE) wrongly insisted that:

- All cancers are caused by an excess of black bile.

- Depressed women are more prone to cancer than cheerful women.

- The liver manufactures blood and the other organs consume it.

- Blood passes through pores in the wall between the two sides of the heart and is mixed with air on the left side.

- The brain—not the sinus passages—manufactures phlegm.

Sight Unseen

In comic books, when Superman uses his X-ray vision to see through concrete walls, X-rays shoot from his eyes. X-rays are merely an energetic form of light, and living creatures do not see by radiating light from their eyes. Instead, light enters the eye and stimulates the nerve cells in the retina. For Superman to see through concrete walls, X-rays reflected from the wall would have to stimulate the nerve cells in the Man of Steel's retinas.

Only Her Hairdresser Knows for Sure

In 1955, when the Foote, Cone & Belding advertising agency launched its campaign for Clairol hair-color products with the catchphrase "Does she . . . or doesn't she?" executives at *Life* magazine, finding lewd connotations in the line, initially refused to run the print advertisements—until a survey showed that women did not fill in the ellipsis with the same lasciviousness demonstrated by men.

Busted

On November 3, 1970, police at Cleveland Hopkins International Airport arrested actress Jane Fonda, who was returning from speaking at an anti–Vietnam War fund-raiser in Canada, for possession of a large quantity of pills. The police dropped all charges after identifying the pills as vitamins.

The Top Ten Reasons Not to Snub Letterman

On September 24, 2008, Republican presidential candidate John McCain canceled a scheduled appearance on the *Late Show with David Letterman*, explaining that he was "suspending his campaign" and "racing to the airport" to return to Washington, D.C., to tackle the nation's looming financial crisis. "This doesn't smell right," Letterman told his viewers. "This is not the way a tested hero behaves. Somebody's putting something in his Metamucil." Halfway through the taping of the show, Letterman learned that McCain was a few blocks away being interviewed by *CBS Evening News* anchor Katie Couric. Showing a live feed of the interview to his viewers, Letterman shouted at the monitor: "Hey, John, I've got a question. Do you need a ride to the airport?"

Titanic Flop

The producers of the 1980 movie *Raise the Titanic*, based on the best-selling novel by Clive Cussler, spent $350,000 to build a faithful, fifty-five-foot model of the *Titanic*. When the finished model turned out to be too large for the studio tank, the producers built a larger tank—at a cost of $6 million. The resulting $40-million movie earned only $7 million at the box office.

The Beagle Has Crash-landed

Beagle 2, Britain's first unmanned Martian space probe, was scheduled to land on Mars on Christmas Day 2003, but instead disappeared without a trace. British scientists suspected that either a Martian heat wave and accompanying dust storms had thinned the atmosphere, causing *Beagle 2* to enter the atmosphere too fast and crash, or the space probe's parachutes and airbags had simply failed to deploy properly—causing the $90-million space probe to be lost forever.

The Fine Print

In 1990, Random House publisher Joni Evans agreed to pay actress Joan Collins $4 million to write two novels, paying her $1.2 million upon signing the contract. Collins turned in manuscripts titled *The Ruling Passion* and *Hell Hath No Fury*, both following the disjointed bedroom antics of two sisters. When Evans labeled both manuscripts "unpublishable," Random House sued to get back its $1.2 million. But Collins argued that her contract required her to submit "complete manuscripts," not "acceptable" ones, entitling her to keep the money and obligating Random House to pay her the remaining $2.8 million for the two complete manuscripts she had submitted—regardless of their coherence. The jury ruled that Collins had written the first book, *The Ruling Passion*, but not the second book, which they deemed a reworking of the first. The judge allowed Collins to keep the $1.2 million and ordered Random House to pay her an additional $925,000, plus interest.

Mighty Big Desk

On February 15, 1980, Republican presidential candidate Ronald Reagan said, "All the waste in a year from a nuclear power plant can be stored under a desk." The average nuclear power plant generates thirty tons of radioactive waste each year.

Married to Their Work

In 1986, the *Stamford Advocate* published a front-page story by Lisa Marie Petersen citing an unpublished, unfinished Harvard-Yale study indicating that college-educated single women at age thirty-five had only a 5 percent chance of ever getting married. The Associated Press picked up the story, prompting every major newspaper and network news program to report the statistics. In response, U.S. Census Bureau demographer Jeanne Moorman used conventional standard-life tables to analyze data from the 1980 census and projected that single women age thirty-five actually had a 32 to 41 percent chance of getting married.

Get Real

In 1977, R.J. Reynolds Tobacco Company nationally introduced Real, a cigarette with no artificial ingredients, without doing any test marketing, and spent $40 million on advertising and free samples—only to discover that smokers are not "health conscious." R.J. Reynolds discontinued Real in 1980.

Casting Aspersions

For the 1939 horror film *The Return of Doctor X*, Warner Bros. studio head Jack Warner cast the droll Humphrey Bogart to star as the vampire-like Dr. X, complete with a pasty white face, an ascot, and a streak of white in his buzz-cut hair. The movie was frightening, but not in the way the studio had intended.

The Puking President

On January 8, 1992, President George Bush, attending a state dinner in Tokyo and suffering from an intestinal flu, vomited into the lap of Prime Minister Kiichi Miyazawa and then collapsed on him—giving birth to the Japanese word *bushuru* ("to vomit publicly").

Signs of Intelligence

While signing his name in cement in front of Grauman's Chinese Theatre on Hollywood Boulevard in September 1981, actor Burt Reynolds misspelled his name.

We Do Chicken Wrong

On May 5, 2009, talk show host Oprah Winfrey promoted KFC's new grilled chicken on her show and invited viewers to visit a Web site to download a coupon for a free two-piece Kentucky Grilled Chicken meal with two sides and a biscuit. Millions of viewers downloaded the coupon and went to the nearest KFC to redeem it, but KFC, having underestimated Oprah's influence, was unprepared for the overwhelming response. Havoc ensued. Some franchises told customers that the promotion was over for the day, others insisted that the offer stood only "while supplies last," others limited the offer to the first one hundred customers, and still others said that coupons with bar code numbers ending in 1234 were invalid (only the coupon for the free two-piece chicken meal ended in 1234). Oprah apologized on air for the commotion, and KFC offered to provide a free Kentucky Grilled Chicken meal plus a medium soft drink to those who submitted the original coupon. On June 17, two dissatisfied customers filed a class-action suit against KFC, claiming the giveaway was a "bait and switch" operation to dupe people into spending money at the chain.

All Things Being Equal

In a fund-raising letter sent out in July 1992, television evangelist Pat Robertson said the equal rights amendment "is about a socialist, anti-family movement that encourages women to leave their husbands, kill their children, practice witchcraft, destroy capitalism, and become lesbians." The equal rights amendment stated: "Equality of rights under the law shall not be denied or abridged by the United States or by any State on account of sex."

Is *Pocket* a Euphemism?

In the 1719 novel *Robinson Crusoe* by Daniel Defoe, Crusoe takes off his clothes, swims to a wrecked ship, finds some biscuits, and then, we are told, puts them in his pockets.

Another Meathead

In 1970, actor Mickey Rooney turned down the role of Archie Bunker on *All in the Family*, convinced that Norman Lear's new television show was too harsh for television audiences. Lear cast Carroll O'Connor instead, and *All in the Family* became the number one show on television for five years.

Ms. Diagnosis

When Eleanor Roosevelt, wife of President Franklin Delano Roosevelt, fell ill at the age of seventy-eight and began bleeding and bruising at the slightest touch, her doctors diagnosed that she suffered from anemia. The former first lady actually had tuberculosis. Rather than giving Roosevelt an open bone marrow biopsy to confirm their diagnosis, her doctors began treating her with prednisone, a drug that fights blood diseases. Unfortunately, prednisone also lowers the body's resistance to infection, enabling the undiagnosed tuberculosis to spread faster, ultimately killing Eleanor Roosevelt.

Funny Bones

Three of Russia's most revered saints (Bishop John, Saint Euphemia, and Saint Euphorosynia) lived in the fourteenth century and purportedly protected their communities from Mongolian invaders. For centuries, ancient Russian Orthodox religious centers near Moscow housed the skeletons of the three saints. In 1981, however, Russian forensic experts proved that the remains were actually the bones of Mongolian invaders.

Out of Tune

In 1999, Shawn Fanning developed Napster, a file sharing network that music lovers could use to swap copyrighted music online. The Recording Industry Association of America (RIAA), representing the major record companies, immediately sued Napster for contributing to copyright infringement. In response, Napster CEO Hank Barry suggested that the music industry adopt a radio-style licensing agreement that would pay royalties to artists for music distributed through the Internet. The recording industry refused to partner with Napster, and the Ninth Circuit Court of Appeals in San Francisco prohibited Napster from enabling the swapping of copyrighted music.

Napster aficionados switched their allegiance to other peer-to-peer file sharing networks, and the RIAA sued some thirty thousand music piracy sites, including MP3.com, Gnutella, Grokster, and Kazaa. Today, music-distribution services (such as iTunes), music-subscription businesses, and streaming services (such as Pandora) dominate digital music sales. Had the record companies partnered with Napster and other file sharing networks in 1999, rather than suing them, they might likely control digital music sales today.

On Pins and Needles

In 1849, Brooklyn inventor Walter Hunt invented and patented the safety pin and then sold all the rights to his invention for $400, never receiving another penny for it. A century later, the United States produced an estimated five billion safety pins annually. Hunt died broke in 1859.

Behind the Times

In 1879, British manufacturer Walter Alcock invented the world's first roll of perforated toilet paper. He struggled for the next ten years in Victorian England to mass-produce and market his product to a prudish public that deemed the subject taboo and refused to consider toilet paper's obvious benefits.

Souped Up

On January 1, 1965, actor Soupy Sales told the viewers of his children's television show on New York's WNEW-TV: "Go into your daddies' wallets and remove those little green pieces of paper with pictures of George Washington, Benjamin Franklin, Lincoln, and Jefferson on them. Send them to me, and I'll send you a postcard from Puerto Rico." A viewer filed a complaint with the Federal Communications Commission, and the station suspended the show—for one week.

Facebook Unfriends Yahoo!

In July 2006, Yahoo! offered to buy the two-year-old social network Facebook from 23-year-old creator Mark Zuckerberg for $1 billion.

Created by Zuckerberg while he was an undergraduate at Harvard University, Facebook had eight million members. Mindful that Rupert Murdoch had purchased the social network Myspace, with its 100 million members, for $580 million a year earlier, Zuckerberg agreed to the deal. But shortly afterward, Yahoo!'s projected sales fizzled and its stock price plummeted 22 percent, prompting company head Terry Semel to reduce his $1-billion offer to $800 million. Zuckerberg said no. Two months later, Semel offered the original $1-billion bid, but by then Zuckerberg had decided to keep Facebook. In January 2011, Facebook was valued at $50 billion while Yahoo! was valued at $14 billion.

Tears in Beer

In the 1970s, Schlitz Brewing Co. changed the formula of Schlitz ("the beer that made Milwaukee famous" and then the second-best-selling brand in America), substituting corn syrup for barley and cutting fermentation time to one-third the original time, ruining the original taste. In 1976, the company added new chemicals to stabilize the foam, but wound up creating tiny flakes in the beer. The resulting recall and destruction of an estimated ten million cans of Schlitz killed sales and destroyed the company. In 1981, the Stroh Brewery Company bought Schlitz and moved "the beer that made Milwaukee famous" to Detroit.

Clearing the Air

In 1771, Swedish chemist Carl Wilhelm Scheele (1742–1786) heated mercuric oxide and discovered that the resulting gas is one of two gases that comprise air. Scheele wrote a book, *Chemical Treatise on Air and Fire*, describing his experiments and asked his patron, Swedish chemist Torbern Bergman, to write the introduction. Bergman took so long that the publisher was unable to print the book until 1777, by which time English chemist Joseph Priestley had reported his own experiments and had taken credit for the discovery of oxygen.

Twelve Stupid Things Dr. Laura Did

In 1998, Dr. Laura Schlessinger, host of the number one syndicated talk radio show in the United States and author of the best-selling book *Ten Stupid Things Women Do to Mess Up Their Lives*, dispensed advice on morality, family values, and personal responsibility to eighteen million listeners daily. In October, the Internet Entertainment Group posted on its Web site twelve nude photos, including extremely revealing close-ups, taken of Dr. Laura more than two decades earlier by her former mentor, retired radio talk show host Bill Ballance, thirty years her senior, with whom the self-righteous Schlessinger was forced to admit she had engaged in an extramarital affair.

The Ultimate Dog
and Pony Show

In 1911, British explorer Captain Robert Scott decided to use white
Manchurian ponies to haul his team to the South Pole, despite their
proven vulnerability in Antarctic conditions. After a grueling expedition, Scott and his four companions reached the South Pole on
January 18, 1912, only to discover that Norwegian explorer Roald
Amundsen had beaten them there a month earlier. Amundsen had
wisely used dogs to haul his group. On the return journey, Scott and
his party died from starvation and exposure.

Underestimating the Gravity
of the Situation

In 1687, British mathematician and physicist Sir Isaac Newton
(1642–1727) published his theories of gravity, stating that the gravitational attraction between any two bodies in the universe is
directly proportional to the two masses multiplied together and
inversely proportional to the square of their distance apart. Albert
Einstein disproved this theory, accepted by scientists for 240
years. Newton also based his original theory of the gravitational
force of the earth on a remarkebly inaccurate measurement of
the earth's radius.

Forbidden Fruit

In 1753, Scottish naval surgeon James Lind, having discovered that citrus fruit prevents scurvy, published his findings in his *Treatise on the Scurvy*, urging the British Admiralty to add citrus juice to the naval diet. The British navy ignored Lind's prescription for forty-two years, during which time countless members of the navy suffered from the disease.

Curing Malaria with Jell-O

In 1804, French chemist Armand Seguin erroneously concluded that the ingredient in the bark of the cinchona tree that cures malaria is gelatin. Seguin published his findings, prompting physicians to treat their malaria patients with clarified glue. The ingredient in cinchona bark that cures malaria is quinine. Their patients should have drunk tonic water.

A Matter of Interpretation

On December 29, 1977, when President Jimmy Carter arrived at the Warsaw airport and gave a short speech, his State Department translator, Steven Seymour, speaking a strange mixture of archaic Polish and Russian, mistranslated Carter's statement "I have come to learn your opinions and understand your desires for the future" as "I desire the Poles carnally."

Shakespeare's Mistakes

Something Rotten in the State of Denmark

In *Hamlet*, the ghost of Hamlet's father mentions the Catholic concepts of purgatory and absolution, despite the fact that the play takes place in Denmark at a time when the Danes were pagans. Shakespeare also mentions Elsinore's "beetling cliff." Elsinore, a seaport in Denmark now called Helsingør, does not have any cliffs.

Talking Turkey

In his play *Henry IV, Part 1*, which takes place in 1403, Shakespeare mentions turkeys—creatures that were not brought to Europe from Mexico by the Spaniards until 1519 and which did not reach England until 1524.

Behind the Eight Ball

In Shakespeare's play *Antony and Cleopatra*, which takes place in ancient Egypt, Cleopatra invites others to play billiards, centuries before the game was invented.

Wrong Island, Wrong Wife, Wrong Mother

In his play *Coriolanus*, William Shakespeare incorrectly calls Delphi an island. Delphi, the site of Apollo's oracle, was an ancient Greek town on the southern slope of Mount Parnassus, on the Greek mainland. The playwright makes Virgilia the wife and Volumnia the mother of Coriolanus. According to *Lives of the Noble Greeks and Romans*, written in the late first century by the ancient Greek historian Plutarch, the wife of legendary Roman leader Gaius Marcius Coriolanus was actually named Volumnia and his mother was named Veturia.

The Big Hand

In his play *Julius Caesar*, which takes place in 44 BCE, Shakespeare refers to a clock that strikes the hour—a type of clock that wasn't developed in Western civilization until the late 1200s.

Great Balls of Fire!

In his play *King John*, which takes place in the early thirteenth century, Shakespeare mentions a cannon. Cannons were not invented until the fourteenth century.

Two Truths Are Told

In Shakespeare's play *Macbeth*, Macbeth murders King Duncan asleep in bed. Historically, Macbeth killed Duncan in a battle at Pitgaveny, near Elgin. In the play, Macduff slays Macbeth at Dunsinane. Macbeth actually escaped, and historians credit Macduff's son Malcolm with killing Macbeth at the Battle of Lumphanan, on August 15, 1057.

The Coast Is Clear

In *The Winter's Tale*, Antigonus says, "Our ship hath touched upon the deserts of Bohemia." Bohemia, a fertile plateau in a landlocked region in the Czech Republic, does not have a coast or any deserts.

The Best-Laid Plans
of Wives and Men

In 1986, Sheriff M. G. "Corky" Woodward of Morris County, Kansas, rented a video camera to film his wife and himself making love. When he returned the camera to the store in the town of Council Grove, he accidentally left the ninety-minute, sexually explicit tape inside the camera. When county residents circulated copies of the tape and demanded Woodward's resignation, the sheriff refused to step down. A year later, Woodward finally bowed to pressure and quit. Shortly afterward, the humiliated couple left town.

Elementary,
My Dear Watson

In his 1887 short story, "A Study in Scarlet," Sir Arthur Conan Doyle tells us that Sherlock Holmes's assistant, Dr. Watson, was wounded in the shoulder by a bullet during the war. In his 1890 short story, "The Sign of the Four," Doyle tells us the bullet wound is in Watson's leg.

The Fen-phen Fiasco

In 1979, Michael Weintraub, a professor of clinical pharmacology at the University of Rochester, decided to combine two nonaddictive drugs approved by the Food and Drug Administration—fenfluramine, an appetite suppressant, and phentermine, a stimulant—to create a long-term diet aid to control obesity. After Weintraub successfully tested fen-phen on 121 obese patients for four years, *Clinical Pharmacology & Therapeutics* published his study in July 1992, creating a fen-phen craze. Weintraub, however, overlooked the fact that the Food and Drug Administration had never approved the two drugs to be taken in combination for long periods of time.

In August 1996, a report in *The New England Journal of Medicine* linked the use of fen-phen for more than three months to a twenty-three-fold increased risk of developing primary pulmonary hypertension, a fatal lung disorder. Subsequent studies revealed that prolonged use of fenfluramine can cause heart-valve defects. In September 1997, the Food and Drug Administration ordered fenfluramine to be taken off the market.

So Much for Ballpark Estimates

In 1965, the Long Island Lighting Company projected the cost to build the Shoreham Nuclear Power Plant on Long Island, New York, at $65 million. By the time the plant was completed in 1989, the cost had reached $5.5 billion. When local authorities refused to approve the company's evacuation route for residents in the event of a serious accident, Governor Mario Cuomo and the Long Island Lighting Company announced plans to decommission and dismantle the plant—at a cost of $186 million.

Suriname State of Mind

In 1674, the Dutch traded New Netherland, including New Amsterdam (now known as Manhattan), to Great Britain for Suriname, a small country in South America. In 2008, New York City had a gross domestic product of $1.46 trillion. The Republic of Suriname's gross domestic product for that same year was $4.5 billion.

Shroud of Mystery

In 1357, a shroud stained with a negative, life-size image of what appears to be a bearded, crucified man, believed by many Christians to have been Jesus, surfaced in the tiny village of Lirey, France. Since 1578, the shroud, wrapped in red silk, has been kept in a silver chest in the Chapel of the Holy Shroud in the Cathedral of St. John the Baptist in Turin, Italy, where it has been venerated as the white burial shroud used to wrap the body of Jesus following the crucifixion. In October 1988, with permission from Turin archbishop Anastasio Ballestrero, a team of 250 scientists carbon-tested the shroud and dated it to sometime between 1260 and 1390, providing conclusive evidence that the shroud is medieval.

Going Bananas

In 1986, Silo, a discount electronics store chain, ran a television commercial in Seattle, Washington, and El Paso, Texas, offering a stereo system for "299 bananas." Dozens of customers lined up outside the stores with bags of bananas—compelling Silo to honor the offer, resulting in a loss of $10,465.

Ancient Mistake

In 1987, when archaeologists claimed that a series of petroglyphs discovered on three boulders along the south fork of the Coquille River in the Siskiyou National Forest in Oregon were the work of early tribes, the Forest Service began building an interpretive center—until artist Jeff Kerker admitted that he had innocently carved the petroglyphs fifteen years earlier as an experiment to determine how long it would take to make them.

The Snail Trail

In the 1850s, French immigrant and vintner Antoine Delmas became the first person to bring vine cuttings to California from France. He also brought snails so he would have an ample supply of escargot. The ubiquitous offspring of those original brown *Helix aspersa* snails destroy millions of dollars' worth of California produce every year.

Tea Time

In 1994, the Snapple Beverage Corp. created a craze for its irreverently advertised flavored tea and fruit drinks, prompting the Quaker Oats Company to buy the corporation for $1.4 billion. The Coca-Cola Company and PepsiCo quickly introduced their own tea and fruit drinks, advertising heavily, undercutting Snapple's prices and crushing the brand's sales. Less than three years later, the Quaker Oats Company sold the ailing Snapple Beverage Corp. for $300 million—at a loss of more than $1 billion.

In Case of Resurrection

In March 1992, South Carolina's Greenville County Department of Social Services sent a letter to a dead man that read: "Your food stamps will be stopped effective March 1992 because we received notice that you passed away. May God bless you. You may reapply if there is a change in your circumstances."

Nothing New Under the Sun

In 1886, American inventor Charles Fritts created a working solar cell using the element selenium, but scientists considered him a fraud. Sixty-eight years later, in 1954, after quantum mechanics had discovered how selenium conducts more electricity in sunlight than in darkness, scientists at AT&T Bell Telephone Laboratories developed a semiconductor solar cell.

Mein Dummkopf

German dictator Adolf Hitler promised that his Third Reich would last one thousand years. It lasted twelve years and left Germany completely decimated.

Rescue Gone Askew

In 1970, Special Forces Lieutenant Colonel Arthur "Bull" Simons selected fifty-nine soldiers from the Special Operations Forces and Green Berets and trained them for several months at the Eglin Air Force Base in Florida for a raid to rescue some sixty American prisoners of war from Son Tay prison camp in Vietnam, just twenty-three miles west of Hanoi. On November 20, 1970, Simons and his troops infiltrated Son Tay by helicopter and killed between one hundred and two hundred Vietcong—only to discover that the prison camp had been closed for three months and the prisoners had been moved to another camp.

Dead Set Against It

In 1991, the Sony Corporation sent an invitation to ragtime pianist Eubie Blake, inviting him to attend a special ceremony in his honor where the company would present him with its first Legendary Innovator Award and introduce him to industry people who could help further his career. Blake had died eight years earlier.

Bordering on Stupidity

In 1877, surveyors mapping the western border of South Dakota started from the south and traveled only as far north as the southern border of the Montana territory at the 45th parallel, where a monument was erected to mark to the spot. In 1885, surveyors mapped the eastern border of Montana Territory south from the Canadian border along the 27th meridian, and checked their survey with a line run back to the north—only to discover that the monument marking the southeastern corner of Montana had been built nearly one mile west of the 27th meridian. The surveyors placed a second marker at the actual corner, allowing the western border of South Dakota to jump nearly one mile east-west where it hits the southern border of Montana. South Dakota's western border with Wyoming inaccurately remains a little more than 4,600 feet west of the 27th meridian.

Turning Back Time

In the spring of 1930, Josef Stalin ordered that clocks in the Soviet Union be set ahead one hour for daylight savings time. In the fall, he forgot to order citizens to turn their clocks back again, but no one had the courage to tell the oppressive dictator he had erred. After sixty-one years running one hour ahead of its original time zones, the Soviet government finally admitted the error and agreed to fix it. On March 31, 1991, Russia and most republics in the Soviet Union set their clocks back one hour.

¿Qué Pasa?

On August 7, 1979, a Spanish Air Force Mirage IIIEE jet intentionally fired shells into a hillside practice target site at the Bardenas Reales Firing Range, near Zaragoza, Spain. The shells ricocheted, hitting the engine area and downing the plane. The pilot and crew ejected safely.

The Empress's New Clothes

On June 17, 1999, Columba Bush, wife of Florida governor Jeb Bush, returned to the United States from a trip to Paris and told customs officials at Hartsfield-Jackson Atlanta International Airport that she had nothing to claim. Customs officials inspected her luggage and discovered $19,000 worth of designer clothing and accessories that Mrs. Bush was apparently attempting to smuggle into the country to avoid paying taxes. She claimed that she had lied on her customs form because she didn't want her husband to find out how much money she had spent on her shopping spree in Paris. The U.S. Customs Service slapped Mrs. Bush with a $4,100 fine—three times the duty she owed.

Slaves to Time

In the 1960 movie *Spartacus*, a fictional account of an actual slave revolt against the Roman Empire in the first century BCE, several Roman soldiers can be seen wearing wristwatches.

Spelling Error

During an on-air radio interview in April 1999, shock jock Howard Stern asked actress Tori Spelling, who starred on the hit television show *Beverly Hills, 90210*, to name the capital of New York. Spelling replied, "New Jersey?"

Silly Goose

In 1942, during World War II, shipping tycoon Henry J. Kaiser and millionaire Howard Hughes became partners and received $18 million from the United States government to build a giant seaplane, the HK-1 Hercules, larger than a modern-day 747 and capable of carrying sixty tons of cargo. They began building the world's biggest plane from wood impregnated with resin, but when the project exceeded the original ten-month projection, the government cut its funding. Kaiser quit the partnership, but Hughes invested $7 million of his own money.

Nicknamed the *Spruce Goose* (despite the fact that there was no spruce used), the plane was finished in 1946—a year after World War II had ended. The *Spruce Goose* flew only once and not very well. On November 2, 1947, Hughes took off from Long Beach Harbor, flying just over one mile at an altitude of seventy feet for one minute. The *Spruce Goose* sat in a climate-controlled warehouse in Long Beach, California, until 1993, when it was sold and moved to McMinnville, Oregon, where it can be seen at the Evergreen Aviation & Space Museum.

Luke, Memorize Your Lines

In the 1977 movie *Star Wars*, after Luke Skywalker destroys the Death Star and gets out of his fighter, he shouts "Carrie!" to Princess Leia, played by actress Carrie Fisher.

It's a Bird! It's a Plane! No, It's Naïveté!

In 1938, teenagers Joe Shuster and Jerry Siegel developed the comic book superhero Superman and sold all the rights to their "man of steel" to Detective Comics for a flat fee of $170, never expecting that their creation would become the world's most popular comic book superhero and generate millions of dollars.

The Buck Stops Here

Between January 1979 and March 1980, the U.S. Bureau of the Mint struck 857 million Susan B. Anthony dollar coins—in hopes of saving taxpayers an estimated $50 million a year (since fewer paper dollars would have to be printed) and an additional $100 million (the cost of building a new printing plant). Because of its similarity in size to the quarter and the fact that five out of six Americans opposed a dollar coin, the Susan B. Anthony dollar never caught on with the public, leaving the Federal Reserve with 525 million uncirculated coins in the Department of the Treasury's vaults.

Swine Flu Over the Cuckoo's Nest

On March 24, 1976, President Gerald Ford asked Congress to appropriate $135 million for a federal campaign to inoculate the entire United States population against a virus with swine flu characteristics that had first appeared a month earlier among soldiers at Fort Dix in New Jersey. Vaccinations began in October, resulting in thirty-two deaths and hundreds of lawsuits against the government for adverse reactions, including heart attacks and paralysis. The government ended the program in December 1976.

A Drop in the Bucket

In September 1978, a worker dropped a fifty-five-cent paint scraper into a torpedo launcher of the U.S. nuclear submarine *Swordfish*—costing the U.S. government $171,000 in repairs.

Cross That Bridge Before It Falls Down

In the 1870s, British civil engineer Sir Thomas Bouch designed a two-mile-long bridge to cross Scotland's Tay River from Newport to Dundee. The bridge was opened in 1878, and the following year Queen Victoria awarded Bouch a knighthood. On December 28, 1879, a hurricane hit the bridge, blowing thirteen spans of wrought-iron lattice girders into the river, bringing the Edinburgh mail train with them, killing all seventy passengers aboard. Bouch had neglected to make any provisions for the bridge to withstand the effects of wind pressure or provide any continuous lateral wind bracing below the deck.

Bad Call

On December 28, 1875, inventor Alexander Graham Bell offered newspaper publisher George Brown of Toronto a half interest in all patents that Brown would take out on the telephone outside the United States in return for $50 a month for no longer than six months (so that Bell could perfect his invention and prepare the patent specifications). After agreeing in writing to the deal and making the first payment, Brown changed his mind and let the agreement lapse—afraid that haughty London financiers would ridicule him for being associated with such an impractical invention as the telephone.

Another Ding-a-ling

In 1876, Alexander Graham Bell, having patented the telephone, offered Western Union, then the largest communications company in America, exclusive rights to his invention for $100,000. Western Union president William Orton turned down the offer. An internal memo at Western Union read: "This 'telephone' has too many shortcomings to be seriously considered as a means of communication. The device is inherently of no value to us."

A High-Pressure Situation

On September 25, 1992, NASA launched the $980-million *Mars Observer* to orbit and photograph the planet Mars. On August 21, 1993, three days before the probe was about to go into orbit around Mars, NASA lost contact with it. The resulting investigation revealed that the spacecraft was supposed to have pressurized its fuel tanks five days into the mission, but NASA had postponed pressurization for eleven months to avoid a possible fuel leak. The lack of pressurization for eleven months had likely caused a rupture in the fuel line.

Blind Ambition

In Cecil B. DeMille's 1956 movie *The Ten Commandments*, which takes place sometime around 1200 BCE, a blind man is seen wearing a wristwatch.

Bombs Away

On August 11, 1984, before making a weekly radio broadcast on National Public Radio, President Ronald Reagan jokingly said during a microphone check: "My fellow Americans, I'm pleased to tell you today that I've signed legislation that will outlaw Russia forever. We begin bombing in five minutes." After someone leaked a recording of the comment to the media, the Soviet Far East Army was put on full alert for thirty minutes.

Who Suggested the Suggestion Box?

The Tennessee Valley Authority spent $700,000 to administer a program that rewarded employees for suggestions that saved the utility company money. The TVA ended the program in 1988 because the forty-six implemented suggestions had saved the company only $580,000.

Mexico's Mistake

In 1821, the Mexican government granted Missouri banker Moses Austin permission to establish a colony of Americans in Texas. By late 1825, Austin's son Stephen had brought three hundred American families to Texas and many other Americans had founded colonies there as well. In 1830, Mexico, suspecting the United States of plotting to annex Texas by encouraging Americans to colonize the province, prohibited further American immigration into Texas.

Five years later, the thirty thousand American colonists living in Texas (far outnumbering the three thousand Mexicans living there) severed their ties with the Mexican government to fight for Texan independence. In 1836, the Americans won the war, captured Mexican dictator Antonio López de Santa Anna, and established the independent Republic of Texas, ultimately joining the United States in 1845.

Ring My Bell

Marquis Yi of Zeng, a fifth-century BCE Chinese ruler, was buried in a tomb in the city of Suzhou—with a set of sixty-five bronze bells, forty stringed instruments, and twenty-one young women to play them in the afterlife.

Reacting to Pressure

In October 1978, a pressure relief valve in the cooling system around the core of one of three nuclear reactors at Three Mile Island near Harrisburg, Pennsylvania, began leaking, but the management of the General Public Utilities Corporation, which ran the facility, did nothing to correct it. Around the same time, the Nuclear Regulatory Commission discovered that nine out of 150 pressure relief valves in U.S. nuclear power plants were faulty, but failed to notify any nuclear power plant to check its pressure relief valves. On March 28, 1979, the malfunctioning pressure relief valve at Three Mile Island got stuck open for more than two hours. This mishap allowed thousands of gallons of cooling water to escape, causing the core of the nuclear reactor to overheat to within less than an hour of a meltdown.

Tiptoe Through the Tulips

In the seventeenth century, "Tulip-mania" swept Europe as owning rare breeds of tulips became a status symbol. The middle class, realizing how much money the upper classes spent on tulip bulbs, began breeding the bulbs, which were sold by weight. Traders earned as much as $44,000 a month. In 1637, the same year that three Rembrandt tulip bulbs sold for $25,000, the tulip market crashed and many people lost fortunes. Today a tulip bulb costs roughly fifty cents.

Out of Control

Time magazine printed 200,000 copies of the cover of its March 21, 1983, issue before an employee discovered that the word *control* was misspelled *contol* in a blurb. *Time* executives stopped the presses, corrected the misspelling, and pulled the bad covers—delaying distribution of 40 percent of its newsstand copies by one day and costing the company $100,000.

Dude, I Completely Flaked Out

In 1804, French chemist Armand Seguin discovered a method for extracting morphine from opium, but failed to publish his discovery for ten years. In 1806, German chemist Friedrich Sertürner published his own method and was credited for discovering the innovative technique.

The Tip of the Iceberg

The designers of the "unsinkable" RMS *Titanic* divided the ship into sixteen watertight compartments, which could be sealed shut individually by the flip of an electronic switch. If any two of the compartments flooded, the ship would remain afloat. In the unlikely event that three compartments flooded, the ship would sink. When the *Titanic* hit an iceberg on its maiden voyage just before midnight on April 14, 1912, the resulting 300-foot-long gash opened six of the sixteen compartments. Also, the ship's designers provided only sixteen wooden lifeboats and four collapsible lifeboats—enough to carry 1,178 people—despite the fact that the *Titanic* carried 2,228 passengers and crew. At 2:20 a.m. on April 15, 1912, the "unsinkable" *Titanic* sank.

A Spike in Crime

On May 10, 1869, the Union Pacific and Central Pacific railways were linked together with two golden spikes during a well-publicized ceremony at Promontory, Utah. Although the builders immediately replaced the golden spikes with steel spikes to avoid theft, within a few days souvenir-hunters disconnected the transcontinental railroad at the historic spot, stealing twelve spikes, six ties, and two pairs of rails.

What Goes Around Comes Around

On March 29, 1942, the British warship HMS *Trinidad*, sailing in the Arctic Ocean, fired a torpedo at a German destroyer. The icy waters caused a faulty gyro mechanism in the torpedo to send the torpedo circling back to strike the *Trinidad*, killing thirty-two crewmen and damaging the ship so badly that it had to be taken out of service for the rest of the war.

Not Quite Up to Speed

In the early seventeenth century, Italian scientist Galileo Galilei attempted an experiment to measure the speed of light by using two lanterns on two separate hilltops. The experiment failed because the speed of light is 186,282 miles per second—too fast to be measured from such a short distance.

Playing It by Ear

On June 28, 1997, during the third round of a heavyweight championship boxing match at the MGM Grand in Las Vegas, challenger Mike Tyson bit off a piece of Evander Holyfield's right ear and spit it out on the canvas. The referee disqualified Tyson, and on July 9, the Nevada State Athletic Commission fined the boxer $3 million and revoked his license to fight in Nevada for one year.

Go Figure

In 1969, Chancellor of the Exchequer Roy Jenkins announced that the United Kingdom had underestimated the value of British exports by 2 to 3 percent over the previous six years—amounting to a $1.6-billion accounting error. In other words, the United Kingdom's plummeting trade deficit had never existed in the first place, and the resulting austerity measures that had devastated the economy and lowered the standard of living in Great Britain had been completely unnecessary.

The Persistent Problems of Misogyny

Harvard University repeatedly refused to grant American philosopher and psychologist Mary Whiton Calkins (1863–1930) a Ph.D. because she was a woman, despite the protests of Harvard alumni. Calkins became the first woman president of the American Psychological Association and the author of the book *The Persistent Problems of Philosophy*.

Condom Conundrum

In the 1960s, the United States Agency for International Development shipped a 139-year supply of condoms to Thailand. The condoms had a shelf life of five to ten years.

Ready, Aim, Misfire!

On April 15, 1980, U.S. Air Force pilot Captain Harry Cook, instructed to shoot down an unmanned target plane in a peacetime training mission over Florida, got confused and shot down a manned F-4 Phantom fighter jet instead. The two crewmen parachuted to safety, but the $3.3-million F-4 Phantom fighter crashed into the Gulf of Mexico near Sarasota.

Granting Wishes

On November 20, 1981, U.S. education secretary T. H. Bell announced that the Department of Education, having failed to check the claims made by students about family income and other information, gave away an estimated $300 million in federal grants to undeserving college students for the 1980–81 academic year.

Technically Speaking

In the spring of 1990, the United States Office of Management and Budget announced that estimated tax revenue for the next five years had been based on a Treasury Department accounting error and was $130 billion too high, calling the resulting deficit a "technical re-estimate."

Using His Head

In the final game of the 2006 World Cup (in extra time, with the game tied 1–1), French soccer captain Zinedine Zidane head-butted Italian Marco Materazzi in the chest and was thrown out of the game. Without Zidane, the French team failed to unlock Italy's defense, losing the game 5–3.

The Beauty of Arsenic

As early as the eighteenth century, women in Europe and America ate Arsenic Complexion Wafers to attain a fashionably pale complexion. The advertising copy in the 1902 Sears Roebuck catalogue for Dr. Rose's Arsenic Complexion Wafers explained: "Taken as directed the wafers will be found a positive, safe, and magical specific for all sorts of skin troubles, unsightliness, and imperfections, being in reality the only beautifier of the complexion, skin, and form known." Arsenic whitens the skin by destroying red blood cells. By consuming the poisonous wafers, women risked blindness and death.

Deadly Beauty

In ancient Greece, affluent women colored their cheeks and lips with rouge and lipstick made from cinnabar, a poisonous red sulfide of mercury.

Stamp Out Stupidity

In 1991, the United States Postal Service issued a stamp in honor of former vice president Hubert H. Humphrey. After printing 300 million stamps, the Postal Service discovered that the stamps used "1964 to 1968" as the dates of Humphrey's term in office. Humphrey served as vice president from 1965 to 1969. The stamps were destroyed at a cost of $380,000.

Walking on Thin Ice

Rapper Vanilla Ice, who exploded onto the rap scene in 1990, claimed that he had grown up in the mean streets of Miami, had attended the same high school (Miami Palmetto Senior High) as rapper Luther Campbell of 2 Live Crew, and had won three national motocross championships. Later that year, student journalists at Palmetto Senior High revealed that Vanilla Ice (born Robert Van Winkle) had grown up in a white, middle-class suburb of Dallas, had never attended high school in Miami, and had never won any national motocross championships.

Up in Smoke

In February 2010, London's *News of the World* published a photograph of Michael Phelps, the 23-year-old winner of eight Olympic gold medals, at a South Carolina party smoking from a bong. Consequently, the Kellogg Company, the world's biggest cereal maker, deemed Phelps's behavior inconsistent with its image, refused to renew a lucrative sponsorship agreement with the swimming champion, and donated thousands of boxes of Corn Flakes cereal featuring the athlete's picture to a San Francisco food bank.

Stayin' Alive

In *The Aeneid*, Latin poet Virgil (70–19 BCE) recounts the adventures of Trojan warrior Aeneas after the fall of Troy. In that epic poem, Asylas slays Chorinaeus and Nisus slays Numa—but later both Chorinaeus and Numa reappear as if they had never been killed.

Who's Counting?

On November 7, 2000, all the major television networks covering the presidential election projected Al Gore the winner in Florida, and then, within an hour, retracted that call. The networks had all relied on erroneous data from Voter News Service (VNS), an exit-polling and vote-counting service that claimed Gore had captured an astonishing 96 percent of the votes in Florida's Duval County. Hours later, the networks declared George W. Bush the winner in Florida and the president-elect, but two hours later retracted that call as well, saying the race was too close to call. VNS had entered more erroneous data into its system, prematurely giving Bush the victory.

You Better Watch Out

Around one o'clock on Christmas morning in 2003, a naked man got stuck in the chimney at Uncle Hugo's Bookstore in Minneapolis. At nine a.m., a passerby heard screams coming from inside the store and called the police. Firefighters rescued the 34-year-old man by breaking the chimney with sledgehammers. Police suspected that the nude man had been drunk when he climbed onto the roof of the one-story building and took off his clothes in hopes of squeezing through the chimney. Police charged the naked man with attempted burglary.

Turning the Tables

In the late 1980s, movie director Guy Ritchie was fired from his job as a furniture mover after he tied an antique table to the roof of his van and drove through a low tunnel, destroying the piece.

Deserting a Sinking Ship

On April 15, 1912, the *Wall Street Journal* reported, "The gravity of the damage to the *Titanic* is apparent, but the important point is that she did not sink." The *Titanic* had sunk hours earlier.

Fumble

In 1989, the Minnesota Vikings, determined to acquire a world-class running back in hopes of winning the Super Bowl, gave the Dallas Cowboys five players and seven future draft picks in exchange for Heisman Trophy winner Herschel Walker. The deal enabled the Dallas Cowboys in 1992 to acquire University of Florida running back Emmitt Smith, who helped them win the Super Bowl in 1993, 1994, and 1996. The Vikings, meanwhile, cut Walker from the team in 1991.

War and Aging

In the 1869 novel *War and Peace*, by Russian author Leo Tolstoy, Natasha Rostova is seventeen years old in 1805. Four years later, in 1809, she is twenty-four years old—having miraculously aged seven years. Also, Prince Andrei possesses a silver icon that inexplicably turns to gold later in the novel.

The Illegal President

The United States Constitution states that the president of the United States must be a natural-born citizen or a citizen at the time the Constitution was adopted on July 21, 1788; must be at least thirty-five years old; and must have resided in the United States for fourteen years (Article II, Section 1). Since the United States came into existence on July 4, 1776, no one could have been considered a fourteen-year resident of the United States until July 4, 1790. George Washington was elected president in 1788 and inaugurated on April 30, 1789—fourteen months before he was constitutionally permitted to assume the office.

Just a Matter of Time

On July 4, 1848, the day the cornerstone was laid for the Washington Monument, a zinc-lined time capsule was placed inside the foundation. No one recorded exactly where the time capsule was buried. It has never been found.

Do Not Enter

In 1915, the *Washington Post* reported that President Woodrow Wilson had attended the theater with his fiancé, Edith Galt, but was more occupied entertaining her than watching the play. A typographical error in the story made a pivotal sentence read: "The President spent most of his time entering Mrs. Galt."

A Dirty Movie

The 1995 movie *Waterworld*, made for a record $175 million, bombed at the box office. In the film, the earth is completely submerged in water, yet all the people, living in small boats on the water in the sun, are covered with dirt and grease.

Catch His Drift

In 1912, German climatologist and geophysicist Alfred Wegener asserted in his book *The Origin of Continents and Oceans* that a supercontinent he called Pangaea had started breaking apart 200 million years earlier and that the pieces had drifted to their present positions. Geologists ridiculed Wegener's ideas—until the 1950s, when scientists began to understand plate tectonics and realized that is exactly what happened.

The Bad Rhythm Method

In 1986, bookstores received copies of *First Love: A Young People's Guide to Sexual Information* by popular radio sex adviser Dr. Ruth Westheimer. Three months later, the publisher, Warner Books, discovered that the book incorrectly told readers that a woman will not get pregnant if she has intercourse during the week before ovulation. In fact, a woman having intercourse during this time is most likely to get pregnant. Warner Books recalled the 115,000 copies in distribution and issued a corrected edition with a different-color cover. Surprisingly, no lawsuits resulted from any readers who became pregnant.

Flabbergasted by Flubber

When Walt Disney released the movie *Son of Flubber* in 1963, Hassenfeld Brothers, a Rhode Island toy company known today as

Hasbro, sold more than four million packages of a tie-in product: Flubber, a mixture of rubber and mineral oil somewhat like Silly Putty. When the Flubber caused minor rashes in hundreds of children, Hasbro recalled the product and commissioned a city dump to burn the substance. When the burning Flubber created a huge cloud of black smoke, the city ceased the operation. The Coast Guard then gave Hasbro permission to dump the concoction at sea. The globules resurfaced all over Narragansett Bay. Local fishermen helped round up the Flubber, which was then buried—either in a landfill or, as urban legend holds, under the parking lot of a Hasbro factory.

A Fertile Imagination

Napoleon Bonaparte and his wife Josephine, married in 1796, were crowned emperor and empress of France in 1804, but the couple failed to conceive an heir to the throne. Since Josephine already had two children, Napoleon remained convinced that he was infertile—until his mistress, Eléonore Denuelle, became pregnant with his child.

Flight of Fancy

In June 1990, the press discovered that Virginia governor Douglas Wilder had flown on a state-owned airplane to visit Nantucket with former model Patricia Kluge, who, under the stage name Patricia Rose, had starred in the 1969 soft-porn movie *The Nine Ages of Nakedness*. Earlier that year, Wilder had appointed Kluge, who had recently separated from billionaire John Kluge after nine years of marriage, to the board of visitors of the University of Virginia. Wilder reimbursed the state $3,707 for the plane trip and insisted that he and Kluge were simply "friends."

Here She Comes, Miss America

On September 17, 1983, Vanessa Williams became the first African American to win the Miss America title. Unbeknownst to the pageant organizers, a few months earlier Williams had posed nude for photographer Tom Chiapel, for whom she worked as a receptionist. When the lewd pictures surfaced in the September issue of *Penthouse* magazine, pageant officials forced Williams to relinquish the Miss America crown.

Hot Crockery

In 1977, Random House published *Woman's Day Crockery Cuisine*, a cookbook that included a recipe for "silky caramel slices." The recipe instructed readers to heat an unopened can of evaporated milk in a Crock-Pot, but accidentally neglected to tell readers to fill the pot with water. When Random

House discovered that following the recipe could cause the can of evaporated milk to explode, the publisher recalled ten thousand copies of the cookbook.

Jell-O Spies

In July 1950, the FBI arrested 32-year-old electrical engineer Julius Rosenberg as a spy for the Soviet Union. According to the FBI, Rosenberg had torn a Jell-O box top in half, given a piece to his brother-in-law, David Greenglass, and told him that his contact at Los Alamos National Laboratory would produce the other half. The contact turned out to be spy courier Harry Gold, who received atomic-energy data from Greenglass and paid him $500, allegedly giving the Soviet Union the secret of the atom bomb. Although Rosenberg insisted on his innocence, he and his wife, Ethel, were sentenced to death in 1951, and after several appeals, on June 19, 1953, the Rosenbergs became the first Americans ever executed for using Jell-O.

A Turn for the Worse

On June 28, 1914, when Archduke Franz Ferdinand, heir to the throne of Austria-Hungary, and his wife, Sophie, arrived in Sarajevo, the capital of the Austrian province of Bosnia, a man threw a bomb at their chauffeured royal touring car, but accidentally hit another car instead. Rather than making a scheduled visit to a museum, Ferdinand decided to go to the hospital to visit the men injured by the bomb. Unfortunately, no one informed the chauffeur about Ferdinand's change in plan. The chauffeur followed the planned route to the museum, and when instructed to turn the car around, he stopped in front of Gavrilo Princip, a young Bosnian student allied with the bomb thrower. Princip jumped on the running board of the car and shot Ferdinand and Sophie with a pistol—resulting in the outbreak of World War I.

Blitz on the Fritz

On February 22, 1940, a German fighter plane flying off the coast of Borkum strafed, bombed, and damaged two destroyers—the *Lebrecht Maass* and the *Max Schultz*. Both ships belonged to the German navy.

The Point of No Return

On February 26, 1993, terrorists rented a Ryder van to transport a bomb that they detonated in the garage of the World Trade Center in New York City, destroying the van. Afterward, one of the terrorists, Mohammed Salameh, made four visits to the Ryder truck rental office in Jersey City, New Jersey, claiming that the van had been stolen and demanding that his $400 deposit be returned. The FBI, having found among the debris a fragment of the van containing the vehicle identification number, traced the van back to the Jersey City office and arrested Salameh there on March 4, 1993.

Salameh had rented the truck using his real name, address, and phone number, and his receipt was impregnated with traces of the explosives the terrorists had used.

Oops! Wrong Way!

On July 16, 1938, pilot Douglas Corrigan took off in an airplane to fly solo nonstop from New York to Los Angeles. Twenty-six hours later, he landed in Dublin, Ireland. Corrigan explained that he had followed the wrong end of his compass needle and, flying through fog and heavy cloud cover, could not identify any landmarks.

Bug Off

In the twentieth century, computer developers programmed millions of computers and software using only two numbers (rather than four) to represent the figure for the year. Computers would read the digits 99 as 1999, but when the calendar year turned to 2000, experts feared that computers might read 00 as 1900. Television and radio pundits predicted disastrous scenarios. To avoid the possibility that computers might recalculate interest on mortgages, empty bank accounts, negate insurance payments, or cause planes to fall from the sky, governments and businesses upgraded their computers at an estimated cost of $100 billion. Panicked citizens stocked up on canned goods. On January 1, 2000, no major catastrophes were reported.

Close Before Striking

In 1892, Joshua Pusey, a lawyer from Lima, Pennsylvania, invented the matchbook—foolishly placing the striking surface inside the front cover, enabling the slightest friction to cause the entire matchbook to go up in flames.

Welcome to . . . Huh?

In 1517, when Spanish explorer Francisco Hernández de Córdoba arrived on what is now known as Mexico's Yucatán Peninsula, he asked the Mayan Indians what they called their land. The Mayans replied, "Yucatán," which translates to "I don't understand what you're saying."

Space Cadets

In October 1964, grade school science teacher Edward Mukuka Nkoloso, director of Zambia's National Academy of Science, Space Research, and Philosophy, pledged that his country would beat the United States and the Soviet Union to the moon. Twelve prospective Zambian astronauts were trained by being spun around in fifty-gallon oil drums hung from the end of a rope and by learning to walk on their hands, which, Nkoloso told *Time* magazine, is "the only way humans can walk on the moon."

Getting the Message

In the event the United States entered World War I, German foreign minister Arthur Zimmermann hoped to get Mexico to attack the United States in exchange for Germany's help in recapturing Texas, New Mexico, and Arizona. On January 16, 1917, Zimmermann telegrammed this proposition in code to the German ambassador in Washington, D.C., to be relayed to the German minister in Mexico. British intelligence intercepted and decoded the telegram, and President Woodrow Wilson shared its contents with the American people on March 1, uniting public opinion against a hostile Germany and enabling the president to persuade Congress to declare war on Germany on April 6. Within eighteen months Germany lost the war and signed an armistice.

Who's Your Daddy?

On May 29, 2001, the manager of Chuy's Mexican restaurant in Austin, Texas, called 911 to report two minors attempting to purchase alcohol with fake ID. Police showed up on the scene and arrested nineteen-year-old twin sisters Barbara and Jenna Bush, the daughters of recently inaugurated U.S. president George W. Bush. The judge ordered Barbara, a rising sophomore at Yale University, to pay court fees of $100, serve eight hours of community service, and attend an alcohol awareness course. Jenna, having pleaded no contest to another alcohol-related charge earlier that year, was ordered to pay $600 and perform thirty-six hours of community service. The University of Texas student faced a mandatory jail sentence if she broke the state's underage-drinking law again within the next three months. Her father had signed the bill creating the three-strikes law when he was governor of Texas.

Bringing Home the Bacon

In April 1626, 65-year-old British philosopher and statesman Francis Bacon, attempting an experimental method of preserving meat, stuffed a dead chicken with snow, caught pneumonia, and died.

Space Case

In 1973, Frenchman Claude Vorilhon founded the Raelian movement, a religious group with forty million members worldwide, after he allegedly encountered a flying saucer and spoke with a four-foot-tall alien, who renamed him Rael. Raelians believe that aliens created mankind on the earth thousands of years ago and these aliens now want us to build them an embassy in Jerusalem and invite them to return to earth so we can learn from each other. So far, they have yet to RSVP.

Acknowledgments

At Plume, I am grateful to my editor, Becky Cole, for her unbridled enthusiasm for this book. I am also deeply thankful to ace copy editor Kym Surridge, designer Daniel Lagin, assistant editor Nadia Kashper, my agent Stephanie Tade, researcher Debbie Green, my manager Barb North, and marketing wizard Joel Goldman. Above all, all my love to Debbie, Ashley, and Julia.

Acknowledgments

Sources

"Abruptly, a U.S. Student in Mideast Turmoil's Grip" by Robert D. McFadden, *New York Times*, October 7, 2000

"Air Force Says Jet Shot Down by Mistake" by Associated Press, *Lawrence Journal-World*, August 25, 1981

The Alaska Almanac: Facts About Alaska, 30th Edition by Nancy Gates (Portland, Oregon: Alaska Northwest Books, 2006)

Alexander Graham Bell by Catherine Mackenzie (Whitefish, Montana: Kessinger Publishing, 2003)

"Ambassadors Outraged by Hitler Billboard on Pattaya Highway" by Maxmilian Wechsler, *Bangkok Post*, October 18, 2009

American Boundaries: The Nation, The States, The Rectangular Survey by Bill Hubbard Jr. (Chicago: University of Chicago Press, 2009)

America's Stupidest Business Decisions: 101 Blunders, Flops, and Screw-ups by Bill Adler Jr. (New York: Quill, 1997)

"Amtrak's Web Site: Going Your Way, However Far Out" by Jane Costello, *Wall Street Journal*, April 12, 2000

"Artist Says 'Ancient' Petroglyphs His Own Work" by the Associated Press, *Bangor Daily News*, October 25, 1990

"Asteroid Is Expected to Make a Pass Close to Earth in 2028" by Malcolm W. Browne, *New York Times*, March 12, 1998

"Asteroid Will Miss Earth by 'Comfortable Distance' in 2028," NASA Jet Propulsion Laboratory Press Release No. 9825, March 12, 1998

Backlash: The Undeclared War Against American Women by Susan Faludi (New York: Crown, 1991)

"Biden's Debate Finale: An Echo From Abroad" by Maureen Dowd, *New York Times*, September 12, 1987

The Blunder Book by M. Hirsh Goldberg (New York: Quill, 1984)

Blunders in International Business by David A. Ricks (Malden, Massachusetts: Wiley-Blackwell, 1999)

The Book of Lists by David Wallechinsky, Irving Wallace, and Amy Wallace (New York: William Morrow, 1977)

The Book of Lists 2 by Irving Wallace, David Wallechinsky, Amy Wallace, and Sylvia Wallace (New York: William Morrow, 1980)

"Books: Damsels in Distress" by Paul Gray and Andrea Sachs, *Time*, February 19, 1996

"BSE Test on Sheep Ends in Fiasco" by Charles Clover, *Telegraph*, October 19, 2001

"Bush: Wife Meant to Hide Shopping Spree from Me" by Jo Becker, *St. Petersburg Times*, June 22, 1999

"Butz Resigns," *Michigan Daily*, October 10, 1976

"By George, It's Blarney O'Leary Admits Resume Is False, Quits Irish" by Dick Weiss, *New York Daily News*, December 15, 2001

"Calling Story of Boy and Balloon a Hoax, Sheriff Seeks Felony Charges" by Brian Stelter, *New York Times*, October 18, 2009

Chambers's Journal of Popular Literature, edited by William and Robert Chambers, Volume 34, Number 340 (1860), page 61

The Changing Earth: Exploring Geology and Evolution, 5th Edition by James S. Monroe and Reed Wicander (Belmont, California: Brooks/Cole, 2009), page 474

"Colonel Sanders' March on China" by Carlye Adler, *Time*, November 17, 2003

David Wallechinsky's 20th Century: History with the Boring Parts Left Out by David Wallechinsky (New York: Little, Brown & Company, 1995)

"Detroit's Uphill Battle" by Alexander Taylor, Christopher Redman, and Barrett Seaman, *Time*, September 8, 1980

"Disgraced Cloning Expert Convicted in South Korea" by Choe Sang-hun, *New York Times*, October 26, 2009

"Disgraced Cloning Scientist Hwang Woo-suk Guilty of Embezzlement" by Ju-min Park, *Los Angeles Times*, October 27, 2009

"Drug Company Conducted 'Secret Recall' of OTC Pain Relievers, State Lawsuit Claims" by Gabriel Miller, *Anesthesiology News*, Volume 37, Number 3 (2011)

"Electrical Wiring Configurations and Childhood Cancer" by Nancy Wertheimer and Ed Leeper, *American Journal of Epidemiology*, Volume 109, Number 3 (1979), pages 273–284

Encyclopedia of Earth and Space Science, Volume 1 by Timothy Kusky (New York: Facts on File, 2010), pages 466–468

The Enemy Within: A History of Spies, Spymasters and Espionage by Terry Crowdy (Oxford: Osprey Publishing, 2008)

Exploring Cuzco by Peter Frost (Bucks, England: Bradt Enterprises, 1984)

"The Exposure of a Scientific Fraud" by Norman Swan, *New Scientist*, December 3, 1988

"15,000-Year-Old 'Graffiti' Scrubbed" by the Associated Press, *Newsday*, March 22, 1992

The Film Encyclopedia by Ephraim Katz (New York: Perigee, 1979)

"Football Victory Proves Costly" by Reuters, *New Straight Times*, August 11, 1993

Fumbling the Future: How Xerox Invented, Then Ignored, the First Personal Computer by Douglas K. Smith and Robert C. Alexander (New York: William Morrow, 1988)

Government by Gunplay, edited by Sid Blumenthal and Harvey Yazijian (New York: Signet, 1976)

A History of American Foreign Policy, 2nd Edition by Alexander DeConde (New York: Charles Scribner's Sons, 1971)

"How Can Amazon Tame Controversy over Book on Pedophilia?" by Marjorie Kehe, *Christian Science Monitor*, November 12, 2010

"How Fen-Phen, A Diet 'Miracle,' Rose and Fell" by Gina Kolata, *New York Times*, September 23, 1997

"How Mark Zuckerberg Turned Facebook into the Web's Hottest Platform" by Fred Vogelstein, *Wired*, September 6, 2007

"I Blew It, Perot Says—He Didn't Buy Up Microsoft When He Had a Chance In '79" by Paul Andrews and Stephen Manes, *Seattle Times*, June 14, 1992

" 'I Did a Bad Thing,' Contrite Grant Tells Leno" by the Associated Press, *Toledo Blade*, July 12, 1995

"In Tally of '91 Income, President Lost to Both the I.R.S. and His Dog" by Michael Wines, *New York Times*, April 16, 1992

"Intelligencer: Eubie Blake: Dead Men Don't Wear Tuxes" by Jeannette Walls, *New York*, February 25, 1999

"Intelligencer: Once Upon a Time, There Was . . . S&M" by Jeannette Walls, *New York*, September 2, 1991

"Is Rush Hooked?" by Alex Tresniowski, *People*, October 20, 2003

"It Ain't Over Till It's Over . . . Cold Fusion" by Jerry E. Bishop, *Popular Science*, August 1993

"Jail the Beardstown Ladies!" by Daniel Kadlec, *Time*, March 30, 1998

"Jesse Jackson Reveals Affair, Child" by Larry Copeland, *USA Today*, January 19, 2001

"Joan Collins to Get Additional Million" by Associated Press, *New York Times*, March 1, 1996

"Jon Stewart's 'Rally to Restore Sanity' Drew 200,000, Beating Estimated Attendance at Glenn Beck's" by Meena Hartenstein, *Daily News*, October 31, 2010

"Label Error Led to Cow Brain Mix-up" by Charles Clover, *Telegraph*, December 1, 2001

"Lights Out for Shoreham" by Kinsey Wilson, *Bulletin of the Atomic Scientists*, June 1992

Marilyn Monroe by Barbara Leaming (New York: Three Rivers Press, 1998)

"McLendon's Wife Hit by His Shot" by the Associated Press, *Milwaukee Journal Sentinel*, April 14, 1979

Medical Blunders: Amazing True Stories of Mad, Bad, and Dangerous Doctors by R. M. Youngson and Ian Schott (New York: New York University Press, 1996)

Military Intelligence Blunders by John Hughes-Wilson (New York: Carroll & Graf Publishers, 1999)

"'Millie's Book' Sends Bushes' Income Soaring" by Douglas Jehl, *Los Angeles Times*, April 16, 1992

"Mills Admits Being Present During Tidal Basin Scuffle" by Stephen Green and Margot Hornblower, *Washington Post*, October 11, 1974

"The Missing Links: Piltdown Man" by L. Harrison Matthews, *New Scientist*, April 3, 1981

"Mistake Switches Surgery on Pair" by the Associated Press, *Modesto Bee*, March 18, 1980

Modern Times: The World from the Twenties to the Nineties by Paul Johnson (New York: HarperCollins Publishers, 1991)

"Moonlighting as a Conjurer of Chemicals" by Natalie Angier, *New York Times*, October 11, 2010

"NASA Capsule with Solar Particles Crashes in Utah" by Brian Handwerk, *National Geographic News*, September 8, 2004

"National Affairs: Boston Curtis," *Time*, September 26, 1938

"Networks Say They Must Rethink Their Projections" by Martha T. Moore, *USA Today*, January 5, 2001

"The 1992 Campaign: New York; Clinton Admits Experiment with Marijuana in 1960s" by Gwen Ifill, *New York Times*, March 30, 1992

Now It Can Be Told: The Story of the Manhattan Project by General Leslie R. Groves (New York: Harper & Brothers, 1962)

"Obituaries," *Los Angeles Times*, January 25, 2000

On Leprosy and Fish-Eating: A Statement of Facts and Explanation by Jonathan Hutchinson (London: Archibald Constable & Co., 1906)

"Oops! A Horribly Regrettable Mix-up" by *Time*, March 31, 1980

Oops!: A Stupefying Survey of Goofs, Blunders & Botches, Great & Small by Paul Kirchner (Los Angeles: General Publishing Books, 1996)

The Oxford Companion to English Literature, 4th Edition, edited by Sir Paul Harvey (Oxford: Clarendon Press, 1973)

Panati's Extraordinary Origins of Everyday Things by Charles Panati (New York: Harper & Row, 1987)

"'Pedophiles Guide' Author Arrested in Colorado" by Keith Coffman, Reuters, December 20, 2010

"Pee-Wee Herman Caught in Florida Adult Playhouse" by Karen Dillon, *Hendersonville Times-News*, July 28, 1991

"Pentagon Confirms Soviets Were on War Alert" by *Pacific Stars and Stripes*, October 14, 1984

"Penthouse to Publish Williams" by United Press International, *Altus Times*, July 20, 1984

"Physician Linked to Fake Research" by the Associated Press, *New York Times*, October 10, 1986

The Piltdown Forgery by J. S. Weiner (Oxford: Oxford University Press, 1954)

"Pizza Hut Didn't Deliver, Loses Contract" by Dana Fields, Associated Press, *Free Lance-Star*, January 24, 1997

"Postal Service Sticks with Flawed Stamp," *Los Angeles Daily News*, February 3, 2000

Reader's Digest Book of Facts: Essential and Intriguing Information About This Odd World Around Us by Robert Dolezal (Pleasantville, New York: Reader's Digest, 1987)

Regret the Error: How Media Mistakes Pollute the Press and Imperil Free Speech by Craig Silverman and Jeff Jarvis (New York: Sterling, 2007)

"A Review: The Strange Career of the 'Harvard-Yale Study'" by Andrew Cherlin, *The Public Opinion Quarterly*, Volume 54, Number 1 (1990), pages 117–124

Riding the Roller Coaster: A History of the Chrysler Corporation by Charles K. Hyde (Detroit: Wayne State University Press, 2003)

"Robertson Letter Attacks Feminists," *New York Times*, August 26, 1992

"Rob Lowe's Tale of the Tape" by Michelle Green, *People*, March 19, 1990

"Rush Limbaugh Arrested on Drug Charges" by Jarrett Murphy, *CBS News*/Associated Press, April 28, 2006

Scientific Blunders: A Brief History of How Wrong Scientists Can Sometimes Be by R. M. Youngson (New York: Carroll & Graf Publishers, 1998)

A Short Course in International Marketing Blunders by Michael D. White (Novato, California: World Trade Press, 2002)

"The Smoking Gun Skeleton Mystery" by John Tidey and AAP, *Melbourne Age*, June 27, 1974

"Soupy Sales Dies at 83; Slapstick Comic Had Hit TV Show in 1960s" by Elaine Woo, *Los Angeles Times*, October 23, 2009

Starring John Wayne as Genghis Khan: Hollywood's All-Time Worst Casting Blunders by Damien Bona (Secaucus, New Jersey: Citidel Press, 1996)

Strange Stories, Amazing Facts: Stories That Are Bizarre, Unusual, Odd, Astonishing, and Often Incredible by Reader's Digest editors (Pleasantville, New York: Reader's Digest, 1976)

"The 10 Biggest Blunders Ever in Business" by Melanie Lindner, *Forbes*, March 25, 2008

"'Thalidomide Doctor' Guilty of Medical Fraud" by Robert Milliken, *Independent*, February 20, 1993

Time Almanac Reference Edition 1994 (Washington, D.C.: Compact Publishing, 1994)

"The U.S. Psychic Spy Network" by Jack Anderson and Jan Moller, *Lawrence Journal-World*, December 24, 1996

"Wages of Silence: Milli Vanilli Loses a Grammy Award" by Jon Pareles, *New York Times*, November 20, 1990

"Wedding Party May Have Shot Down Airliner" by the Associated Press, *Herald-Tribune*, October 31, 1986

"The Whistleblower" by Ross Kerber, *Boston Globe*, January 8, 2009

"White House Dandy Recipe: Call It Macaroni" by Ann Cooper, *Baltimore Sun*, December 16, 1981

"White House Pen Pal," *Newsweek*, March 22, 1982

The World Almanac and Book of Facts 1993 (Mahwah, New Jersey: World Almanac Books, 1993)

The World Almanac and Book of Facts 1998 (Mahwah, New Jersey: World Almanac Books, 1998)

The World Almanac and Book of Facts 2000 (Mahwah, New Jersey: World Almanac Books, 2000)

The World Book Encyclopedia by World Book editors (Chicago: World Book, 1985)

World's Worst Aircraft (New York: St. Martin's Press, 1976)

About the Author

Debbie Green

JOEY GREEN got Barbara Walters to make Green Slime on *The View*, got Jay Leno to shave with peanut butter on *The Tonight Show*, got Rosie O'Donnell to mousse her hair with Jell-O on *The Rosie O'Donnell Show*, and had Katie Couric drop her diamond engagement ring in a glass of Efferdent on *Today*. He has been seen polishing furniture with Spam on *Dateline NBC*, cleaning a toilet with Coca-Cola in the pages of the *New York Times*, and washing his hair with Reddi-wip in *People*. Green, a former contributing editor to *National Lampoon* and a former advertising copywriter at J. Walter Thompson, is the author of more than forty-five books, including *Contrary to Popular Belief, Marx and Lennon: The Parallel Sayings, The Zen of Oz, Sarah Palin's Secret Diary,* and *You Know You've Reached Middle Age If . . .* , to name just a few. A native of Miami, Florida, and a graduate of Cornell University, he wrote television commercials for Burger King and Walt Disney World, and won a Clio for a print ad he created for Eastman Kodak. He backpacked around the world for two years on his honeymoon, and lives in Los Angeles with his wife, Debbie, and their two daughters, Ashley and Julia.

Visit Joey Green on the Internet at www.joeygreen.com